Seismology:
OUR VIOLENT EARTH

Essential Library

History of Science

An Imprint of Abdo Publishing | www.abdopublishing.com

Seismology:
OUR VIOLENT EARTH

by Roberta Baxter

Content Consultant

Duncan Agnew
Professor of Geophysics
Scripps Institution of Oceanography

History of Science

www.abdopublishing.com

Published by Abdo Publishing, a division of ABDO, PO Box 398166, Minneapolis, Minnesota 55439. Copyright © 2015 by Abdo Consulting Group, Inc. International copyrights reserved in all countries. No part of this book may be reproduced in any form without written permission from the publisher. Essential Library™ is a trademark and logo of Abdo Publishing.

Printed in the United States of America, North Mankato, Minnesota

02014
012015

Cover Photos: Shutterstock Images
Interior Photos: Shutterstock Images, 1, 3, 63; KSK Imaging/iStockphoto, 7; Arindam Banerjee/iStockphoto, 9; FXEGS Javier Espuny/Shutterstock Images, 12; Lloyd Cluff/Corbis, 15; Glow Images, 17; H. D. Falkenstein/ImageBroker RM/Glow Images, 20; Keren Su/Corbis, 23; Oxford Science Archive/Heritage Images/Glow Images, 25, 64; Bettmann/Corbis, 28, 33, 61; John Woodcock/DK Images, 30; Encyclopedia Britannica/UIG/Getty Images, 37, 73; James Stevenson/DK Images, 41; Roger Ressmeyer/Corbis, 45; US Government, 48; Gary Hincks/Science Source, 50; Rick Wilking/Reuters/Corbis, 53; AP Images, 59; Wally Fong/AP Images, 56; Jan Woitas/picture-alliance/dpa/AP Images, 55; Image Asset Management Ltd./SuperStock, 66; Mark Garlick/Science Source, 69; Claus Lunau/Science Source, 74; Dorling Kindersley/Thinkstock, 77; Keichi Nakane/The Yomiuri Shimbun/AP Images, 81; Jacob J. Kirk/US Navy/AP Images, 84; Kyodo News/AP Images, 87; The Yomiuri Shimbun/AP Images, 89; Chris Sattlberger/Science Source, 91; USGS, 94; Lacy Atkins/AP Images, 97

Editor: Arnold Ringstad
Series Designer: Craig Hinton

Library of Congress Control Number: 2014943878

Cataloging-in-Publication Data
Baxter, Roberta.
Seismology: our violent Earth / Roberta Baxter.
p. cm. -- (History of science)
ISBN 978-1-62403-565-4 (lib. bdg.)
Includes bibliographical references and index.
1. Seismology--History--Juvenile literature.   2. Volcanism--Juvenile literature. I. Title.
551.21--dc23

2014943878

Contents

Chapter **One**   A Tale of Two Quakes 6

Chapter **Two**   Early Seismic Theories 14

Chapter **Three**   Renaissance Science
                      Tackles Earthquakes 24

Chapter **Four**   Waves and Faults 32

Chapter **Five**   How Are Faults and
                      Earthquakes Related? 44

Chapter **Six**   Magnitude and Intensity 52

Chapter **Seven**   Continental Drift 62

Chapter **Eight**   Plate Tectonics 68

Chapter **Nine**   Other Consequences of Earthquakes 80

Chapter **Ten**   An Evolving Science 90

                      TIMELINE 98

                      ESSENTIAL FACTS 100

                      GLOSSARY 102

                      ADDITIONAL RESOURCES 104

                      SOURCE NOTES 106

                      INDEX 110

                      ABOUT THE AUTHOR 112

Chapter One

A Tale of
TWO QUAKES

$$\frac{a+b}{a} = \frac{a}{b} = 1.618$$

P eople strolled through the streets of Port-au-Prince, Haiti, buying vegetables and fruit for their evening meal from the market stalls along the street. Children played as the scent of cooking evening meals wafted on the city's air.

Suddenly, at 4:53 p.m. local time on January 12, 2010, an earthquake shattered the city. Screams filled the air as homes and buildings collapsed in clouds of dust. People jumped out of cars and ran out of buildings to get to any open space they could find.

The country was home to 10 million people. One-fourth of them lived in the capital city of Port-au-Prince. Hundreds of thousands of people lived in urban slums arrayed along the edges and hillsides of the city. Approximately 3.5 million people were affected by the quake.[1]

Port-au-Prince's dense construction and ramshackle building style left it extremely vulnerable to earthquakes.

Death and Damage

The center of the Haitian earthquake was 16 miles (26 km) from the city.[2] The shaking lasted for less than a minute. Since the depth of the earthquake was shallow, only a few miles below ground level, the energy was released close to the surface. This meant the shaking was severe.

Earthquakes are often followed by smaller tremors called aftershocks. Within a few hours after the initial earthquake, powerful aftershocks caused more damage. An estimated 316,000 people died, many of them from collapsing houses and buildings. Another 300,000 were injured. Approximately 1.3 million people were left homeless. Tent cities of refugees sprang up around Port-au-Prince. Estimates suggested nearly 100,000 houses were destroyed and another 190,000 were seriously damaged.[3]

Another Quake Hits

Just over a month later, on February 27, 2010, an earthquake violently shook parts of South America at 3:34 a.m. Most people in Concepción, Chile, had been sleeping. As the

The Haitian earthquake reduced homes and other buildings to piles of rubble.

earth began shaking, citizens of the city ran into the streets in terror.

The quake was 500 times more powerful than the one that hit Haiti in January. The epicenter of the Chilean quake was two miles (3 km) off the coast, disturbing ocean waters. A tsunami hit the coastal city of Constitución with waves up to 50 feet (15 m) high.[5]

As a result of the earthquake and tsunami, a total of 523 people died and approximately 12,000 were injured. Approximately 800,000 people became displaced or homeless as more than 370,000 houses were damaged or destroyed.[6] Hundreds of aftershocks followed.

Why Did More Die in Haiti?

Even though the Chilean quake was much more powerful, it caused less damage and death than the one that hit Haiti. There are several reasons for this.

First, Chile has a long history of earthquakes. The largest earthquake ever measured hit Chile in 1960. The people of Chile are trained in earthquake response. Even schoolchildren have earthquake drills. People rushed out of their homes and buildings when they felt the first tremors. Haiti was not as well prepared for an earthquake.

Second, the area of Chile that was impacted is not as densely populated as Port-au-Prince. Third, the epicenter of the quake in Chile was farther away than in Haiti. Finally, and perhaps most important, the building codes are much stricter in Chile because of the frequent earthquakes. Haiti had no such building codes. Many people lived in ramshackle homes built from weak concrete and masonry.

Large-Scale Destruction

These two earthquakes provide clear examples of the devastation these natural disasters can cause. Earthquakes are among Earth's deadliest disasters, especially when coupled with the tsunamis they sometimes cause. Most other disasters can be predicted. Weather forecasters can predict when a hurricane will hit. With today's technology, they can even get a close approximation of its strength. People can prepare their homes and businesses for the wind and rain and then evacuate to safety. The conditions that

THE ANGRY EARTH

Paulina Fernandez lived in Santiago, Chile, at the time of the 2010 earthquake. She says, "We were sleeping, and suddenly a strong noise woke us up, like cars being crushed and bombs. . . . I thought the earth was mad with us. Nature showed us her fury."[8] She and her son tried to get downstairs, but at first that was impossible because of the heaving of the building. Once they were out, they saw people on the street with no water, no electricity, and no food. People were searching for family members who had gotten separated.

create tornadoes are well known. Even though towns, buildings, and homes cannot be saved, people can take shelter from a tornado.

But earthquakes give little or no warning. Sometimes a few foreshocks will announce a big one might be on the way. However, earthquakes typically strike in the midst of everyday life.

Seismic networks around the world alert seismologists when a quake has occurred and relay information about its location and strength. Scientists hope to develop techniques to predict earthquakes and provide more warning to affected people. But today, the best defense against these massive natural disasters is to design and build structures that will not collapse when an earthquake strikes.

Many buildings in Chile suffered severe damage, but the overall toll was much less than in Haiti.

Chapter TWO

Early Seismic
THEORIES

$$\frac{a+b}{a} = \frac{a}{b} = 1,618$$

Just like people today, ancient people experienced devastation and fear from earthquakes. They tried to explain them based on their ideas of the world.

Thousands of years ago, most people believed earthquakes were caused by the gods. In the ancient Greek culture of the 500s BCE, an earthquake was said to come from the anger of Poseidon, the god of the sea. When he was furious, he stomped around Earth, causing the ground to shake, heave, and even split open. He was also known as the "Earth Shaker." Supposedly his trident also caused earthquakes when he struck the ground with it. The Greek word used for what we call earthquakes was *seismos*, from which we get the term *seismology*.

In the ancient world, the opening of fissures in the earth led to many different theories.

Thales

Thales of Miletus was known in ancient Greek tradition as one of the Seven Wise Men of Greece. He studied the natural world and sought explanations that did not depend on the emotions of the gods. Unfortunately, his writings have been lost. What is known of his work comes from scientists who followed after him.

Thales was interested in all parts of the natural world. The writings of the ancient Greek philosopher Aristotle explain Thales believed all matter came from water. Since Greece is surrounded by the waters of the Mediterranean Sea and all life is dependent on water, it made sense to Thales that the world would be made of water and that water could change into other forms, such as air and earth. He theorized the ground floated on top of a large primordial ocean.

Greeks were accustomed to tossing, wild waves. Thales proposed earthquakes come from a similar cause—the tossing of the water below the earth causing the ground to shake. Just as a person on the deck of a boat is tossed and shaken by agitated waves, a person on the ground during

Thales believed the motion of water was the root cause behind seismic activity.

an earthquake is shaken and the ground heaves like waves. A fact that seemed to support Thales's theory was that springs of water occasionally formed after an earthquake.

Aristotle

Aristotle, who lived from 384 to 322 BCE, also studied earthquakes. He gathered information on past earthquakes and presented his ideas about their origins. He believed three rules applied to these disasters. First, he said, they occur mostly at night. If they occur during the day, they happen at noon. He also said they tend to happen where there are strong sea currents, caves, or hot springs. Finally, Aristotle said earthquakes occur during spring and autumn.

None of these rules turned out to be true. However, another of his observations, that volcanoes and earthquakes happened together, is correct part of the time.

Aristotle thought fast-moving winds were the ultimate cause of earthquakes. Rain soaks into the earth and the sun causes it to evaporate. That makes wind blow inside caves and passages of the earth and leads to earthquakes. Aristotle compared this to the digestive system inside human beings: "We must suppose the action of the wind in the earth to be analogous to the tremors and throbbings caused in us by the force of the wind contained in our bodies."[1]

Seneca

Seneca, a citizen of ancient Rome, lived more than 300 years after Aristotle. He wrote about other philosophers' ideas, refuted them, and put forth his own ideas. In his work *Naturales Quaestiones* (*Natural Questions*) he writes about a recent earthquake in the Roman city of Pompeii. The quake occurred more than a decade before Pompeii was famously destroyed by a volcano in 79 CE. He asks, "[If] the earth itself stir up destruction, what refuge or help can we look for?"[2] People can protect themselves from storms or enemies and even run away from fire. But there is no protection from an earthquake.

Seneca analyzes the causes of earthquakes. "Let us ask ourselves, therefore, what it is that stirs the earth to its foundation, what moves a mass of such weight, what it is that is stronger than the earth, and that in its violence can shake such a load."[3] He describes how earthquakes can change the ground, elevating some sections while lowering others and even pushing up new islands in the seas.

FOUR ELEMENTS

Ancient philosophers proposed everything was made up of a primary substance that expressed itself in four elements—air, water, earth, and fire. Each element had two main characteristics. Water was moist and cold. Air was moist and hot. Earth was dry and cold. Fire was dry and hot. These elements mixed in different proportions to form the world. For example, a fire produces smoke, a type of air, and ashes, a type of earth. Sap, a sort of water, is released as wood burns. All four elements, then, are present in a wood fire.

Each element or combination of elements could change into something different. The ancient scientists looked for these four elements and their actions to explain the natural world.

In addition to earthquakes, Seneca's *Naturales Quaestiones* also discusses lightning, precipitation, comets, and many other natural phenomena.

He notes that some, including Thales, believed earthquakes came from the actions of water. Seneca argues strongly against this notion. He writes that if the world were supported by water, it would always be in motion, not just during earthquakes. He argues that if such water caused quakes, one would expect the entire world to shake, not just a small area, as happens in actual earthquakes.

Seneca next criticizes the idea that earthquakes are caused by another element, fire. He notes that some philosophers believed fire heats up water underground, causing vapor that shakes the ground. He also discusses another theory, that fire causes explosions underground, creating the heaving and splitting of earthquakes.

Ultimately, Seneca agrees with Aristotle that air is the cause of earthquakes. He believes that when air inside the earth is under pressure from being constricted, it bursts forth with the shakes of an earthquake. He writes that he and others "were convinced that it is only air that can attempt such a feat as the production of an earthquake, for . . . nothing in the whole realm of nature is more powerful, more energetic [than it]."[4]

Chinese Scientists

Ancient people in other parts of the world were also studying earthquakes. Zhang Heng lived in China during the Eastern Han Dynasty in the 100s CE. He was an astronomer and mathematician, but he was also interested in earthquakes. He believed they came from air moving inside the earth.

To assist in his studies, he made a device to detect the direction of an earthquake in 132. The device was a large jar with a lid cast of bronze. Eight dragons decorated the top of the jar, facing the four cardinal directions and the four intermediate directions. Each dragon had a tiny bronze ball in its mouth. Directly below each dragon sat an openmouthed frog, also made of bronze. The inner workings of the device caused a ball to fall from the dragon into the frog's mouth when an earthquake occurred in that direction. In 138, a ball fell into the mouth of the west frog. Days later, news reached Zhang Heng that an earthquake had occurred in a province 400 miles (640 km) west of him.[7] Today, a replica of his seismograph is in the Exhibition Hall of the Museum of Chinese History in Beijing, China.

Ancient people made a significant leap in understanding the world around them. A belief in supernatural causes gave way to the understanding that events in the natural world had natural causes. Still, the specific mechanisms by which these events happened were largely a mystery. The incorrect beliefs of the ancient philosophers went mostly unquestioned for more than 1,000 years. New ideas on earthquakes were not proposed until the Scientific Revolution of the 1600s.

Zhang Heng's seismograph was among the earliest tools humans used to study earthquakes.

Chapter Three

Renaissance Science Tackles EARTHQUAKES

$$\frac{a+b}{a} = \frac{a}{b} = 1.618$$

B y the 1600s, scientists in Europe were analyzing everything around them and developing scientific explanations. The Scientific Revolution had begun. Thinkers tested and doubted the theories and principles attributed to ancient philosophers.

Robert Boyle was a wealthy Englishman who was fascinated by all kinds of science. He kept a detailed journal of weather conditions, including temperature, air pressure, and observations on rain and storms. He is famous for experiments he conducted with air pressure, but on January 29, 1666, another phenomenon

Boyle and other scientists began to scientifically study earthquakes in the late 1600s.

EARTHQUAKE SEASONS AND SOUNDS

English astronomer John Flamsteed became interested in earthquakes after a minor one hit England in 1692 and another one destroyed a town in Sicily, Italy, in 1693. He listed his observations:

+ Earthquakes always happen in calm seasons.

+ A sound is heard before the shaking starts.

+ Earthquakes can be felt at sea, giving the impression of the ship running aground.

+ Some earthquakes are felt only locally but others over a widespread area.

+ Earthquakes are felt more strongly on upper floors and not as much in cellars or first floors.

His first observation was not true, though the second was often true. The last three were all true. The observations led him to believe earthquakes could not be caused by underground explosions. The sound heard before a quake, he thought, must mean earthquakes came from the atmosphere. Flamsteed suspected there might be an unseen explosion in the air.

interested him. He had just arrived at a friend's house outside of Oxford, England. The night was cold and wet. Suddenly the whole house shook. Boyle did not realize at first that it was an earthquake. He wrote that he would not have taken notice of it as an earthquake if the idea had not been mentioned by others.

Boyle was a member of the premier scientific organization at the time, the Royal Society. Another member was mathematician John Wallis. Boyle and Wallis joined together to compile information about the small earthquake that occurred in their area. Wallis informed Boyle he felt the quake but assumed it was simply carts rumbling by in the streets. The two scientists collected information about the weather and what people felt during the quake. They wrote a report for the Royal Society summarizing the weather information and noting the quake was felt more strongly in some areas than in others. This was the first time scientific instruments, in this case thermometers and barometers, were used in studying a quake. Though it is now known that weather has no impact on the occurrence of an earthquake, the use of hard scientific data in studying these events set the stage for more advanced research on quakes.

Lisbon Shattered

An event in 1755 caused all of Europe to pay attention to the ground beneath it. On November 1, Lisbon, Portugal, was devastated by an earthquake and the high waves that followed.

Lisbon was a beautiful city with a main square, several cathedrals, and ornate palaces. An aqueduct built in 1731 brought water into the city. Its population of approximately 275,000 made it one of the largest cities in Europe.[1]

On the morning of November 1, a majority of the population was in the city's churches commemorating the Catholic holiday of All Saints' Day. At 9:30 a.m., a rumbling sound was heard. Then the ground began shaking. People in the cathedrals saw large chandeliers swaying as walls shook. The shaking paused. Then came a second shock, followed by a third.

Fires flared up immediately, ignited by cooking fires and heating stoves. Buildings that survived the quake as well as the rubble of fallen structures began to burn. Many people died in the fires, which continued burning for six days.[2]

The twin horrors of the earthquake and the fires drove much of the population to the seaside. People observed the sea had pulled back an unusual distance from the

The combination of an earthquake, a tsunami, and fires caused mass devastation in Lisbon.

shore, but they did not understand why. The quake, which had struck off the coast, led to a tsunami, which hit Lisbon and wiped out houses and businesses in low-lying areas. Scores of people who had rushed to the seaside were swept out into the ocean and died. An eyewitness, Reverend Charles Davy, said he talked to a ship's captain who thought his ship had struck a rock. Actually, the sensation was caused by the waves of energy from the earthquake passing under his ship. Davy concluded that the "extensive and opulent city is now nothing but a vast heap of ruins."[3]

An estimated 60,000 people died in Lisbon. Most large buildings and 12,000 houses were destroyed. The quake caused damage as far away as Algiers, 685 miles (1,100 km) to the east and across the Mediterranean Sea in Algeria. The tsunami traveled west across the Atlantic Ocean to the Caribbean island of Martinique.[4]

Europeans were amazed by the destruction that hit Lisbon. Many believed the earthquake had been sent by God to punish the wicked, but that seemed to be proven false because many had been killed inside churches, while those who were not attending mass were safe. Philosophers and scientists began exploring reasons for the earthquake.

John Michell's Elastic Waves

The Lisbon earthquake also captured the attention of English astronomer John Michell. Michell gathered information about the Lisbon earthquake and theorized it was caused by waves passing through the ground. His explanation: "Suppose a large cloth, or carpet (spread upon a floor), to be raised at one edge, and then suddenly brought down again to the floor; the air under it, being by this means propelled,

KANT'S THEORIES

German philosopher Immanuel Kant tried to understand how earthquakes could produce damage at a distance from where the center was. He knew that lakes miles away from Lisbon had been swirled and agitated on November 1, 1755. How could that happen at such a distance?

His solution echoed that of Aristotle: underground caverns. However, Kant thought air passing through the underground chambers was not strong enough a cause. He decided explosions, possibly from chemicals present underground, must cause earthquakes. Hot air underground could combust and push through the caverns until ejected in volcanoes. The fire would cause more air to be pulled in, exploding again, and so the whole process was like the ground breathing. His theory placed the caverns parallel to mountain ranges and rivers, so those areas were most at risk for earthquakes.

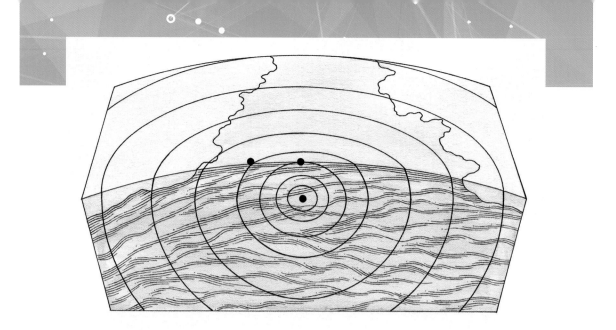

Michell correctly realized the energy of earthquakes moves outward from a central point in waves.

will pass along, till it escapes at the opposite side, raising the cloth in a wave all the way as it goes."[5]

His idea was that a sharp force hitting a point in the earth would travel as an elastic wave, even passing through solid rock. Michell knew sound moves through the air in waves with high points and low points in a regular progression. Properties of sound waves include wavelength, amplitude, and frequency. Wavelength is the distance measured between any point on the wave and the equivalent point on the next wave. Amplitude is the height of the wave from the top to the bottom. Frequency is how many waves occur in a given period of time.

Michell's elastic waves behave much like sound waves. He knew sound waves travel through air, compress, and expand. The elastic waves pass through the rocks as in his carpet analogy. As the waves travel, they cause the earth to vibrate and shake. However, Michell had no explanation for the massive force required to start such a wave.

Using his wave theory and observer reports from Lisbon, Michell calculated the velocity of the wave. It was not an accurate measurement, but it was a start. He figured the waves would go out in all directions, like ripples from a stone dropped in a pond. Michell believed that if one could map the waves, the location of the earthquake could be determined.

His explanation of waves produced by an earthquake and causing the shaking was correct, but he came to the wrong conclusion about the formation of the waves. He noted that earthquakes and volcanoes often occur together, and he thought large fires burning substances such as coal beneath the ground caused rock layers to arch up from the heat. Then pieces of rock would break off and fall into the fire, where the moisture in the rock would explode, causing an earthquake.

Michell tried to fit what eyewitnesses of the Lisbon earthquake reported into a framework that would explain the events. His theory of elastic waves was impressive for its time, but additional information was needed before a more complete theory of the cause of earthquakes could be proposed.

Chapter Four

Waves
AND FAULTS

$$\frac{a+b}{a} = \frac{a}{b} = 1.618$$

B y the middle of the 1800s, scientists were conducting studies with sound waves. They described how such waves form and how they travel. Once scientists realized earthquakes produce elastic waves through the ground, people began investigating the properties of these waves.

The family of Irish engineer Robert Mallet owned a foundry where it built metal supports for bridges, railroad stations, and buildings. In the 1840s, Mallet devised and used a method to investigate elastic waves through the ground using material from one of the family's foundries. On a beach near Dublin, Ireland, he buried a barrel of gunpowder. He lit a fuse to the barrel while he waited with a stopwatch at a safe distance. He also watched a primitive device to show ground movement. It had a

Early seismologists studied how sound waves and elastic waves travel through the earth.

crosshair sight above a drop of mercury. The mercury would move with any ground vibration, showing when the wave arrived at his location.

His experiments showed elastic waves move at different rates through a variety of materials. They moved slower through sand and faster through rock, such as granite. Mallet's work was the first attempt to measure the speed of elastic waves through different substances.

Mallet traveled to Naples, Italy, to observe the aftereffects of an earthquake that hit in December 1857. His report said, "When the observer first enters upon one of those earthquake shaken towns, he finds himself in the midst of utter confusion."[1] However, Mallet looked for patterns in the destruction. He concluded the first movement of the ground would be away from the direction of the earthquake, so objects would fall away from the center. He thought cracks in buildings would also point out the location. Scientists now know the waves produced by earthquakes are very complex, so the direction is not necessarily shown by how debris falls. Also, cracks in buildings are affected more by building materials and techniques than the direction of the earthquake. Still, Mallet's work represented an early effort to collect detailed data about earthquake effects.

Mallet collected magazine and newspaper articles as well as books about earthquakes. He cataloged and mapped earthquakes recorded around the world. His maps were the first to show earthquake-prone areas, and they look much like maps we have today that show where earthquakes and volcanoes occur.

He thought earthquakes were produced by volcanoes, noting they often occur in the same areas. He also thought each quake started from a single point, and he used his observations of the Naples earthquake to estimate it began six miles (10 km) under the surface of the earth.[2]

Mallet made a significant impact on the study of earthquakes with the report he wrote on the Naples quake. He coined the term *seismology* in 1858. He also introduced the term *epicenter*.

Waves of All Kinds

As they learned more about the elastic waves produced by earthquakes, scientists began to identify different types of waves. Seismic waves formed in an earthquake come in several kinds. Two large categories are body waves, which stay underground, and surface waves, which ripple along the surface. The waves spread in every direction from the center of the earthquake, and they carry the energy that causes shaking, heaving, or splitting of the ground. Instruments

SHAKY MISSOURI

The midwestern United States is not known for suffering from severe earthquakes. Yet from December 1811 to February 1812, three large earthquakes and numerous aftershocks rattled the area that is now Missouri.

The quakes were felt as far away as the Gulf Coast, Cincinnati, Ohio, and Quebec, Canada. Landslides and shifting ground completely changed the landscape. The current of the Mississippi River was even driven backward for some hours.

called seismographs measure them, and seismologists use this data to detect where the center of the quake is and how strong it is.

Body waves travel faster than those on the surface, so they are the first to arrive at a seismic measurement site. The P wave, or primary wave, is the fastest and will move through both solid and liquid materials. It works in a push-pull manner, expanding and contracting the rock particles as the energy passes through. Its motion is similar to laying a spring flat on a table and pulling or pushing on one end. The coils will pull apart and then squeeze together as the energy goes from one end to the other. With a P wave, the particles of rock move in the same direction as the wave is going.

Another kind of body wave is the S wave, or secondary wave. It is slower than a P wave and can move only through rock, not through liquid. The S wave is similar to laying a spring flat on a table and moving one end back and forth so that an S shape moves through it.

When the energy of body waves reaches the top of the ground, surface waves form. Surface waves also come in two varieties. One is called the Love wave, named for the scientist A. E. H. Love, who described it in 1912. Love waves force particles back and forth along the top of the wave. Even though these waves do not have up-and-down movement, they cause severe damage by cutting foundations of buildings loose from the ground.

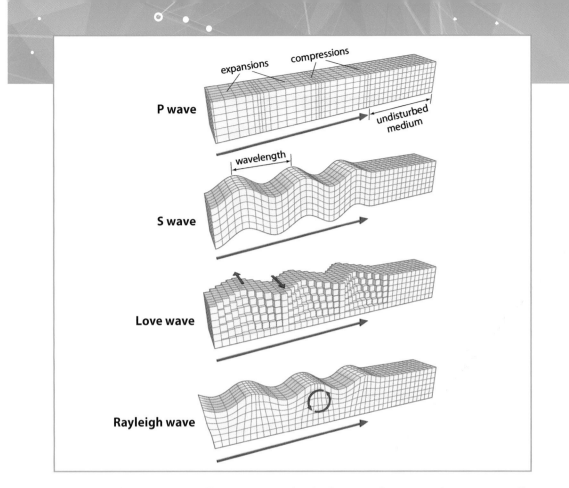

Though surface waves usually move more slowly than P and S waves, they are typically responsible for most of an earthquake's damage.

The other type of surface wave is named Rayleigh waves for John William Strutt, also known as Lord Rayleigh, the English scientist who identified them in 1885. He studied sound waves extensively and transferred his knowledge to earthquake waves.

Rayleigh waves move rock particles in circular motions along the direction of the wave's movement.

Both Love and Rayleigh waves move more slowly than P waves. They travel approximately as fast as S waves or slightly slower, depending on the material through which they pass. Surface waves can travel from the ground into the air, where they are heard as sound waves. This causes the rumbling noise often associated with earthquakes.

Scientists now understood earthquakes consisted of elastic waves passing through the ground. But they still did not know what caused these waves.

How Do Faults Work?

In the 1800s, Sir Charles Lyell of the United Kingdom was known as one of the world's top geologists. He believed the earth changed by extremely slow processes, such as erosion and the buildup of sediment in rivers and lakes. However, he could not explain what was called faulting. Faults can be seen in layered rock. Layers sometimes shift up or down across a fault, showing that one portion of rock had moved in relation to the same layer on the other side of the fault. Miners knew that sometimes a vein of ore would stop but be found again by digging down or up around a fault.

Lyell thought once the rock layers were broken along a fault, they would move independently. After being moved, the layers would line up in a different way than before the rupture happened. But what could cause this to happen? He discovered evidence in New Zealand to support his suspicion that faults break and move.

On January 23, 1855, an earthquake hit the southern part of New Zealand's North Island. The landscape seemed to be pulled apart. Lyell received letters telling him of once-straight streambeds that had been left with bends in them. In some places, the land was lifted higher than the surrounding area. In Wellington Harbor, boat jetties were no longer usable because they had been lifted far above sea level.

In Lyell's famous textbook, *Principles of Geology*, he wrote, "The geologist has rarely enjoyed so good an opportunity as that afforded him by this convulsion in New Zealand, of observing one of the steps by which those great displacements of the rocks called 'faults' may in the course of ages be brought about."[3] Lyell realized faults and earthquakes went together, as other scientists had suspected. But he had not yet determined the cause-and-effect relationship between them. Do faults cause earthquakes, or do earthquakes cause the faults to break apart?

Early scientists did not know why earthquakes occurred in certain places, as shown on Mallet's earthquake map. Lyell's description of faults

Three Types of Faults

Seismologists recognize three basic types of faults. A normal fault has only vertical movement. One side thrusts upward compared with the other. Another kind is the thrust fault. In this case, the rocks of one side of the fault ride up over the rocks of the other side. The third type is a strike-slip fault, in which the ground moves in opposite directions on each side of the fault but does not move up or down. Sometimes movement at a fault can be a combination of these types.

advanced the understanding of why earthquakes happen along faults. Sections of Earth's crust are pushing against each other all the time along fault lines. When the stress becomes too strong, the rocks break apart and slip past each other, sending out waves in an earthquake. The break in the rocks is called a rupture, and it can be feet or miles underground. The spot where the earth begins to rupture underground is the hypocenter of the quake.

Detecting Earthquakes

Besides trying to figure out what caused earthquakes, scientists wanted to detect and compare the strengths of earthquakes. In the 1700s, researchers used a weighted pendulum that would swing with the motion of the ground during an earthquake. There was no way to directly record the motion, but observers could witness the motion of the pendulum—the more it swayed, the stronger the ground movement of the earthquake. However, the data became less accurate with stronger earthquakes.

In 1856, Italian researcher Luigi Palmieri built an electric system that worked better than the pendulum alone. It was a combination of detectors for sideways and up-and-down motion. When movement caused a spring to move, the spring allowed a point to touch a bowl of mercury, which connected an electric circuit. That would cause a clock to stop, giving a time stamp, and it started a pencil marking on a paper, showing the length of the earthquake. Palmieri's setup provided more information than just a pendulum, but it was not very sensitive.

Palmieri's seismograph added time measurements to seismographs, providing seismologists with valuable data.

A group of British scientists working together at the University of Tokyo invented an improved pendulum seismograph. They used a horizontal pendulum style designed by James Ewing in 1880. One of the Englishmen, Thomas Gray, added a spring to the vertical pendulum. The spring made the mechanism more sensitive. Using both horizontal and vertical pendulum seismographs, their system could detect only strong earthquakes. The design also allowed scientists to record an earthquake's motion, the time at which it occurred, and its duration.

In Germany, astronomer Ernst von Rebeur-Paschwitz built a sensitive horizontal pendulum to measure changes in Earth from the movement of other planets. On April 18, 1889, he saw his sensitive instrument swing wildly in a series of peaks. He wondered about the event, but he did not realize what he had measured until months later. An article in *Nature* magazine described an earthquake in Japan just hours before he saw the vibrations. He had recorded seismic waves from the other side of the world.

Later seismographs were vastly more sensitive. Russian inventor Boris Galitzin developed an electromagnetic system in 1906. When movement of the earth is detected, a mass wrapped with wire moves inside a magnetic field produced by a magnet. The magnetic field produces a current in the wire. The current allows the ground movement to be amplified by hundreds of thousands of times compared with the older seismographs, giving a more accurate reading of the size of the earthquake. Seismographs today record digital data for easier recording and manipulation by computer.

One of the British scientists at the University of Tokyo was John Milne. He helped develop the seismograph and decided a network of seismic instrument stations would be valuable in tracking earthquakes. In 1895, he moved back to England and settled at Shide Hill House near Newport. He encouraged placement of seismographs on every inhabited continent. He began gathering seismograph readings from around the world and compiling them into what were called "Shide Circulars."[4]

His work provided seismologists with more information about earthquakes than ever before. His circulars showed earthquakes occurred in unexpected places and in higher numbers than scientists suspected.

Seismologists understood much more about the elastic waves of earthquakes and their relationship with faults. But the 1900s would bring even more important discoveries about the true nature of earthquakes.

HOW DOES A SEISMOGRAPH WORK?

Seismographs need to measure ground movement in three directions: up and down, east and west, and north and south. Three seismographs are used to capture all this information. One uses a weight hung from a spring to measure vertical movement. The other two are situated to monitor movement sideways from east to west or north to south. The combination of the three will detect movement in all directions. A seismograph records the movement on a turning drum so the magnitude of the quake can be seen and time marks are included. Today's seismographs work digitally, but the basic concept is the same.

Chapter Five

How Are Faults and Earthquakes RELATED?

As the 1800s were ending, seismic networks spread around the world. Seismographs became more advanced. John Milne could plot the arrival of the P wave from an earthquake, and in 1900 Richard Oldham identified the S wave from the lines on a seismograph. The P wave arrives first, and each type of wave causes different patterns on a seismograph. By measuring the time interval between the P wave and the S wave measured at three different stations, a seismologist can find the epicenter of an earthquake. The epicenter will be at the intersection of the readings from the three stations.

$$\frac{a+b}{a} = \frac{a}{b} = 1,618$$

Studying fault lines brought about a better understanding of not just earthquakes, but also the very structure of Earth.

TO THE CENTER OF THE EARTH

British geologist Richard Oldham used earthquake waves to study the interior of Earth. He compiled information from numerous earthquakes and noticed P waves were slowed as they traveled deep inside Earth. S waves were delayed even more. In 1906, he theorized the waves were entering a central core that slowed the waves. Other seismologists went on to propose the speed of the waves differed because Earth's core was liquid. The waves move faster through the rocks of the crust but slow down when they hit the liquid core. In 1936, Danish seismologist Inge Lehmann discovered from her studies of seismic waves that there was evidence of a solid inner core inside this liquid core.

In 1897, the first earthquake observatory in North America was established at Lick Astronomical Observatory. The University of California operated it on Mount Hamilton near San Jose, California. As the astronomers studied stars, seismologists watched for earthquakes. They soon had a great deal to observe.

Shaking San Francisco

On April 18, 1906, an earthquake occurred that led to a leap in the understanding of the causes and results of quakes. San Francisco, California, had developed into a beautiful city with stately buildings and lavish homes. At 5:12 a.m., before most people were awake, a foreshock occurred, lasting approximately 20 seconds. Then the tremors and shaking of the earthquake began. People were jolted from their beds. Buildings swayed and toppled, and pieces of them plunged to the streets. Most of the city hall's walls were destroyed, leaving only the metal girders standing. Houses broke from their foundations and leaned against neighboring houses. The fierce shaking lasted approximately one minute and was felt as far north as Oregon, as far south as Southern California, and as far east as Nevada.

The earthquake happened when the San Andreas Fault ripped open for 267 miles (430 km). In many sites, the displacement was as much as 15.5 feet (4.7 m).[1] The fault runs along California and extends as far as 12 miles (20 km) below the surface.[2] The western side is forced northward while the east side is pulled southward. Stress builds up along the fault until it bursts forth with the release of energy in an earthquake.

Brick buildings and those with masonry facades collapsed or shed bricks, killing many people. Another major source of damage stemmed from what was called "made land." When people wanted to build on a marsh at that time, they filled in the marsh with sand and debris to provide a dry surface for construction. This land is unstable, and a process called liquefaction can happen as a result of the shaking of the earthquake. The sand and debris is watery in the lower layers of this made land. The shaking of an earthquake causes water-saturated particles to lose contact with each other and act like water rather than solid ground. The Valencia Street Hotel, built on made land, sank during the earthquake, leaving only the fourth floor above ground.

EYEWITNESS TO THE 1906 SAN FRANCISCO EARTHQUAKE

A local newspaper editor wrote a vivid description of his experience during the San Francisco earthquake:

Of a sudden we had found ourselves staggering and reeling. It was as if the earth was slipping gently from under our feet. Then came the sickening swaying of the earth that threw us flat upon our faces. We struggled in the street. We could not get on our feet. Then it seemed as though my head were split with the roar that crashed into my ears. Big buildings were crumbling as one might crush a biscuit in one's hand.[3]

Nearly 100 people were killed.[4] Earthquake damage was greatest where fill had been added.

Between 3,000 and 5,000 people died in the San Francisco earthquake, many from falling debris.[5] The worst of the damage was yet to come. Fires caused by the earthquake raged for three days. To avoid giving San Francisco a reputation as an earthquake-prone city, officials referred to the entire event as the "great San Francisco Fire." However, the truth of the earthquake was already out.

The existence of the San Andreas Fault had been known since it was discovered and named by geology professor Andrew Lawson in 1895. But no one knew the length of it—more than 800 miles (1,300 km)—until the 1906 earthquake.[6] One of the big questions after the San Francisco earthquake was why the San Andreas Fault existed. What caused it to run down the length of California? Were there unseen faults in other places? Scientists sought to learn more about what powered the motion of the faults.

Harry Fielding Reid, a geologist, was chosen to serve on a group tasked with studying the San Francisco earthquake.

The 1906 earthquake and the subsequent fire destroyed most of the city in what remains among the deadliest disasters in US history.

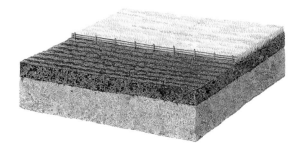

Before earthquake

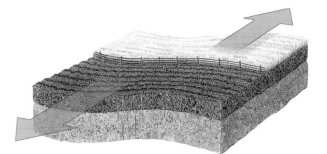

Strain pulls
rocks apart

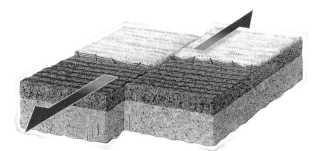

Rocks are
ripped apart

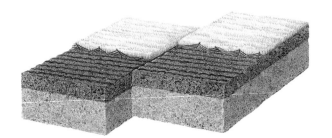

Rocks rebound
to original shape,
separated by
the distance the
fault slipped

The area had been extensively surveyed, so Reid resurveyed sections of land around the San Andreas Fault. From previous surveys, he knew that in fences built across the fault, the fence posts far away from the fault shared movement before the earthquake, demonstrating the strain building up in the fault. The rocks were being deformed under the strain. During the earthquake, the posts near the fault moved as the fault jerked loose, as the friction that causes the sides to stick to each other was overcome by the strain. After the earthquake, the fence sections were separated by the distance the fault had slipped.

Reid called this elastic rebound. The rocks are compressed or expanded under the stress of the fault movement, until the stress is relieved by the movement of the sides of the fault. Then the rocks rebound into their original shape.

Elastic rebound leaves the surrounding rocks in their original shapes but in new positions.

HOW DEEP?

In 1913, German seismologist Beno Gutenberg studied the timing of the travel of seismic waves. His research led him to conclude the depth of Earth's solid core from the surface of the crust was approximately 1,800 miles (2,900 km).[7] His measurement is still considered accurate today.

The top layer of Earth is the crust, made up of rocks and soil. The second layer is called the mantle; this is where earthquakes and volcanoes originate. The mantle is a hot, gooey mixture of magma, made up of partially melted rocks and minerals. Its uppermost section is known as the asthenosphere. The core is the deepest layer and has two parts—a liquid outer core, consisting primarily of liquid nickel and iron, and a solid inner core, made up mostly of iron.

Chapter Six

Magnitude
AND INTENSITY

$$\frac{a+b}{a} = \frac{a}{b} = 1.618$$

When an earthquake occurs, one of the first questions observers ask is "How strong was it?" Seismologists worked for years to find ways to accurately measure and compare the strength of earthquakes. The magnitude of an earthquake is a measurement of the energy released, and it can be measured by the peaks shown on a seismograph. Another measurement of an earthquake is intensity, which measures the strength of the shaking of the earthquake. Intensity varies widely by location.

Two scientists, Michele de Rossi in Italy and François-Alphonse Forel in Switzerland, independently developed intensity scales. De Rossi created his in 1874, and Forel made his in 1881. Once they realized they were both working on the same idea, they cooperated on what became the Rossi-Forel scale.

Scientists interpret data from seismographs to assign magnitude measurements to earthquakes.

MEASURING QUAKES

People often use the terms magnitude and intensity interchangeably when talking about earthquakes, but they are different characteristics. Magnitude measures the size of the earthquake, while intensity measures the severity at a particular location. Intensity is measured by the amount of damage and destruction found, and it varies with distance from the epicenter. An earthquake will feel less intense dozens of miles from its epicenter, but it still has the same magnitude. Both measurements are valuable to seismologists and others, including insurance agents who want to know what damage might have occurred.

The scale ranged from barely perceptible shaking, a 1, to total destruction, a 10. Other scientists adopted the scale, but Giuseppe Mercalli thought he could improve on it by adding more detailed descriptions. The Mercalli scale requires investigators to go to the site of the earthquake and observe the damage. Then the Mercalli ratings can be assigned. One difficulty with the system is that the level of damage may indicate weak construction methods rather than a strong earthquake. If stringent building codes are observed, the damage will be less, leading to a lower Mercalli rating.

One of the greatest challenges for measuring and comparing the size of earthquakes was equipment. Seismographs were still being developed and were not very sensitive. The scales were hampered by the fact that the available instruments were more accurate at measuring strong earthquakes than those of lesser magnitude. They were also better at measuring nearby earthquakes than those that were far away. As instruments became more sensitive, seismologists adjusted their measurements accordingly.

Measuring the magnitude and intensity of earthquakes gives scientists helpful data for studying earthquake causes and effects.

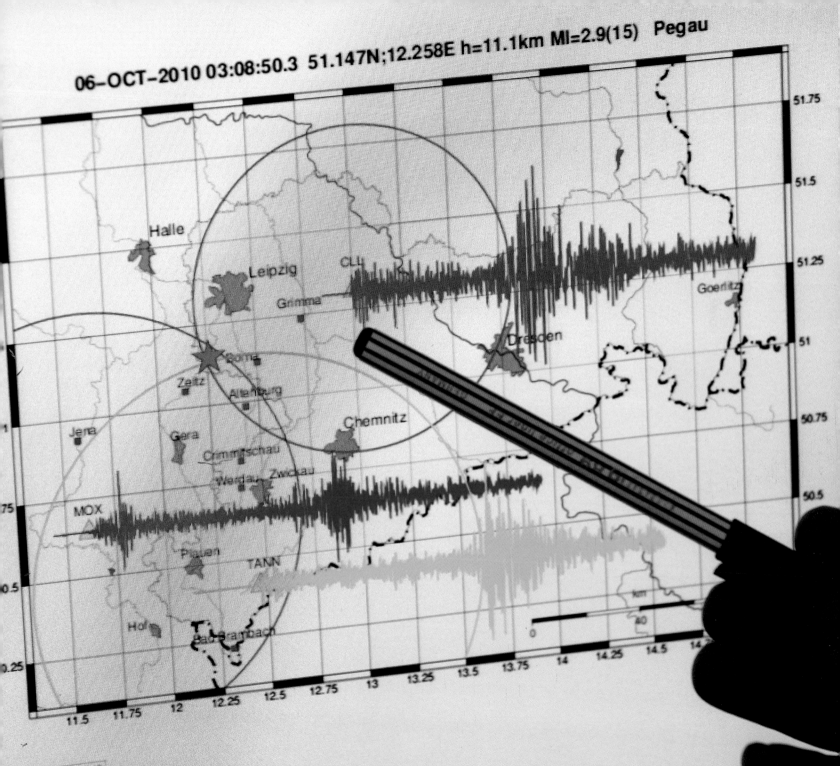

Charles RICHTER

Charles Richter was born in Ohio but grew up in Los Angeles, California. He studied physics at Stanford University and then went on to earn a doctorate at Caltech. When offered a job in the seismology department, he accepted it and began developing the idea of the Richter magnitude scale with colleague Beno Gutenberg.

In 1941, Richter and Gutenberg published a paper called "The Seismicity of the Earth." Richter also wrote the book *Elementary Seismology*, later published in book form and used for decades as a study tool by seismology students. Richter advocated stringent building codes to prevent deaths in earthquakes. He and his wife had no children, but his wife often pointed out to visitors that her husband had a seismograph in their living room.

The Richter Scale

By the 1930s, the man whose name would be forever attached to earthquake magnitude was working at the California Institute of Technology, also known as Caltech. Charles Richter came to Caltech with a degree in physics, but he was soon working in the seismology department. His first tasks involved measuring seismograms and locating earthquakes to compile a catalog of data. In a later interview, Richter said he began thinking about comparing earthquakes by the height of the waves on a seismograph, adjusted by the distance away from the epicenter.

He began trying to plot different magnitudes based on the seismic energy released, but it was difficult because this amount of energy ranged so widely. The range between the largest and smallest magnitudes was huge. Fellow Caltech professor Beno Gutenberg had immigrated to the United States and had a flash of insight about the numbers. He recommended they plot the magnitudes logarithmically. On a logarithmic scale, an increase of one in the magnitude number corresponds to an increase of ten times in the size of the earthquake. An earthquake with a magnitude of 5 is ten times more powerful than one with a magnitude of 4 and 100 times more powerful than one with a magnitude of 3.

EARTHQUAKE MOMENT

Two problems exist with the Richter scale. First, it does not work well for large, distant earthquakes. Also, it is inaccurate measuring earthquakes that occur deep inside the earth.

A Japanese-American scientist working in California, Hiroo Kanamori, created the moment magnitude scale in the 1970s. It measures the work done by moving a section of land for a certain distance. The measurement is obtained by multiplying the average distance of the slip on the fault by the fault area. The moment magnitude scale is abbreviated as Mw.

Richter and Gutenberg began testing their scale on local California earthquakes. Together, they developed what became known as the Richter magnitude scale in 1935.

The Richter scale is still synonymous with seismology today. It is commonly heard in news reports about earthquakes, even though it was later replaced in scientific use by the moment magnitude scale.

Being able to assign magnitudes to earthquakes gave scientists the opportunity to compare the relative strength of the quakes. It also made it possible to predict the level of damage by comparing an earthquake to previous quakes of the same magnitude. Yet when Richter and Gutenberg established their scale, the causes of earthquakes were still unknown. Scientists sought to understand Earth's structure and how it led to devastating earthquakes.

Though newer scales have replaced it, the Richter scale is still the best-known way to measure the strength of earthquakes.

Deadliest Quakes

The most powerful earthquakes are not always the deadliest. Factors that impact the death and damage toll include how highly populated an area is, how strong the construction of local buildings is, and whether tsunamis or fires follow the earthquake. This chart shows several of the deadliest earthquakes.

Location	Number of People Killed	Date
Shaanxi, China	830,000	1556
Haiti	316,000 (includes deaths from a tsunami)	January 12, 2010
Tangshan, China	242,769	July 27, 1976
Sumatra	227,898 (includes deaths from a tsunami)	December 26, 2004
Haiyuan, China	200,000	December 16, 1920
Kanto, Japan	142,800 (includes deaths from fires)	September 1, 1923
Ashgabat, Turkmenistan	110,000[1]	October 5, 1948

A 1976 earthquake brought massive devastation to the city of Tangshan, China.

Chapter Seven

Continental
DRIFT

$$\frac{a+b}{a} = \frac{a}{b} = 1,618$$

Even after the relationship between faults and earthquakes was identified, seismologists still wondered what was powering the movement. In the early 1900s, progress in other scientific fields began bringing these answers into focus.

People had noticed a close fit between the shapes of Africa's western coast and South America's eastern coast. They seem as though they would fit together like pieces of a jigsaw puzzle. Some scientists hypothesized the continents were moving. But others thought this was impossible.

More clues came into the picture as geologists discovered identical rock types existed in South America and Africa, right where the pieces would fit together. New information from the field of biology added another clue. A plant group known as Glossopteris was found fossilized in Australia, India, Africa, South America, and

Theories about continental drift brought radical changes to the way people thought about the structure of Earth's crust.

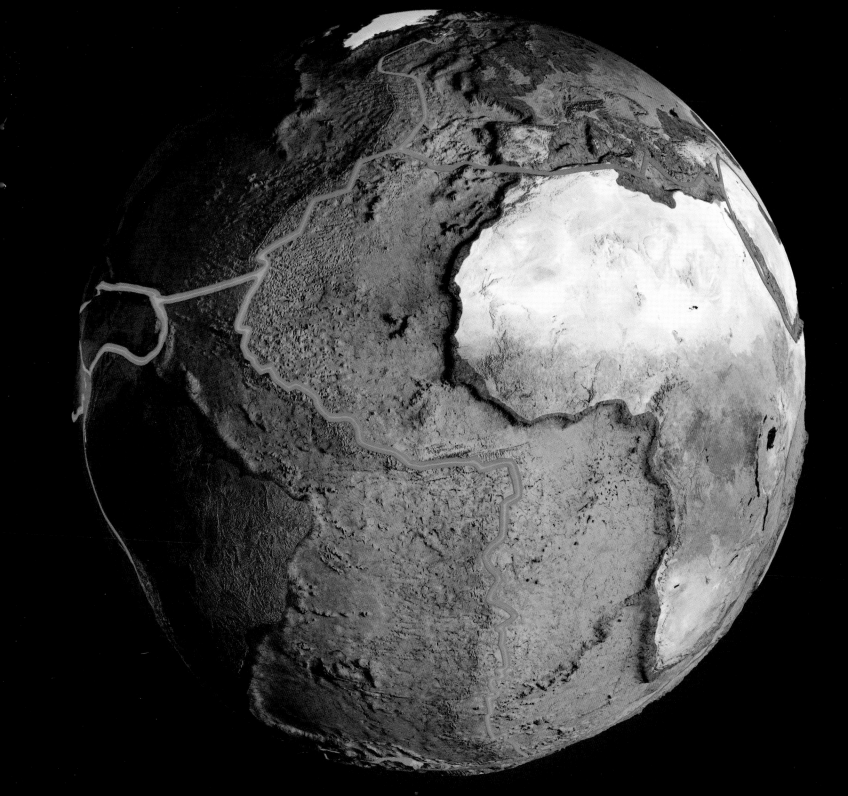

Antarctica. These regions are thousands of miles from each other today, and their current climates vary widely. But somehow this type of plant had survived in all these places at some point in the distant past.

Wegener and Continental Drift

A new idea to explain these strange phenomena came from an unexpected source. Alfred Wegener of Germany was a meteorologist, not a seismologist or geologist. In 1910, in a letter to his future wife, he wrote: "Doesn't the east coast of South America fit exactly against the west coast of Africa, as if they had once been joined? This is an idea I'll have to pursue."[1] He went on to do just that.

Wegener found scientific papers theorizing South America and Africa had once been joined by a land bridge that sank into the sea. He dismissed the idea because no evidence of giant land bridges existed. But if the continents had once fit together, how did they move apart? In January 1912, Wegener attended a meeting of the Geological Association of Germany and submitted his theory that the continents moved and the seas widened. He realized his ideas were revolutionary. Still, he did not think this meant they should be discounted. He wrote to his father-in-law asking, "Why should we hesitate to toss the old views overboard?"[2]

In rejecting the idea of a land bridge, Wegener proposed that originally there was one combined landmass that included all the continents. He called this supercontinent Pangaea, meaning "all lands." Wegener believed Pangaea existed

Alfred WEGENER

Alfred Wegener was born in Berlin, Germany. He earned a doctoral degree in astronomy, but he chose to enter the field of meteorology instead. He used kites and balloons to study the upper atmosphere. On an expedition to Greenland in 1906, he was the first to study the polar atmosphere with balloons.

He accepted a position as a professor of meteorology and wrote a textbook on that subject. His continental drift theory brought him condemnation, but he continued studying polar weather and glaciers, making two more trips to Greenland. On his fourth expedition, in 1930, a party became stranded and Wegener set out to bring them supplies. Wegener and another man got the supplies and set out to return to base camp, but they were not seen again. Wegener's body was found six months later.

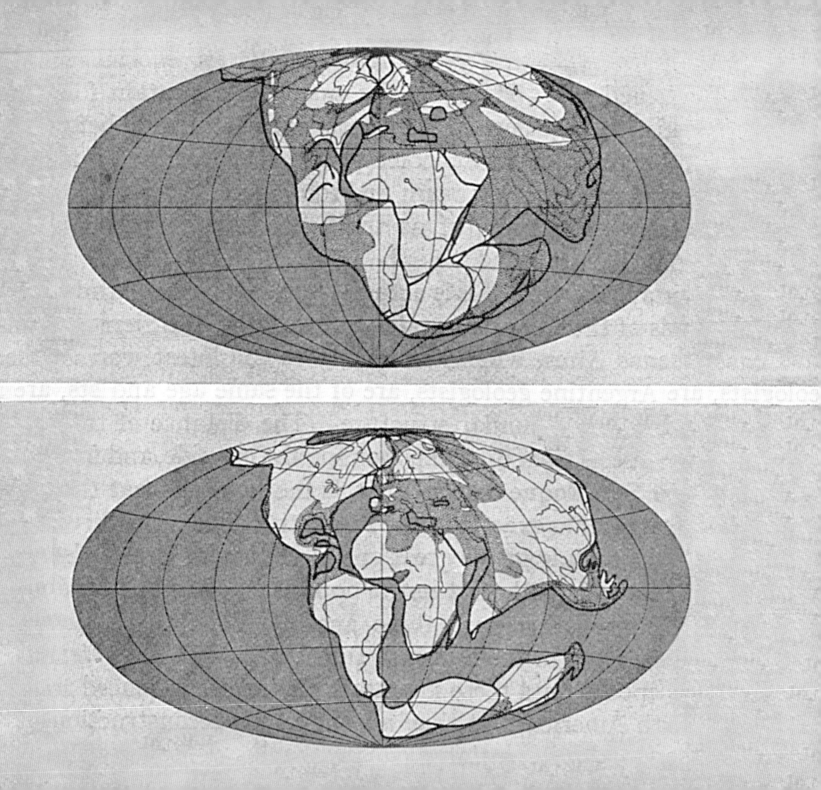

around Earth's South Pole. It split into continents, and they started drifting apart. His theory was called continental drift.

Wegener had stirred up the scientific community with his ideas, but most experts ridiculed his proposal. His status as a meteorologist hindered the acceptance of his theory because geologists viewed him as an outsider.

One missing element in Wegener's theory was the source of power for the movement of the continents. Wegener suggested the centrifugal force of Earth's rotation might drive the separation. He also proposed the movement of continents could be caused by the gravitational pull of the sun and the moon. Both of his theories were criticized because neither mechanism would provide enough energy to move massive continents.

He continued his work on other scientific pursuits, but he still thought about the continental drift theory. After World War II (1939–1945), new technologies would provide information that made scientists reconsider Wegener's ideas.

In drawings accompanying his articles, Wegener showed how he believed continental drift occurred.

SCATHING CRITICISM

Wegener's continental drift theory faced contemptuous reviews from other scientists. The president of the American Philosophical Society said, "Utter, damned rot!" Another American scientist remarked, "If we are to believe [this] hypothesis, we must forget everything we have learned in the last 70 years and start all over again." A British geologist stated that anyone who "valued his reputation for scientific sanity" would not dare support the theory.[3]

These voices all spoke against continental drift, but as later events showed, they were wrong. Eventually, overwhelming evidence forced them to reverse their positions and support a theory based on Wegener's ideas.

Plate
TECTONICS

$$\frac{a+b}{a} = \frac{a}{b} = 1.618$$

B y the middle of the 1900s, scientists were grappling with whether the continents moved and what could power such movement. By 1930, English scientist Arthur Holmes thought the continents were transported on rafts of rock and moved by the process of convection. In this process, lower materials heat up and rise to the top. Materials nearer the surface cool and sink down. Scientists knew temperatures rise deep beneath Earth's surface. Holmes proposed heated material inside Earth was circulating by convection and carrying the continents along with it as it rose and sank.

The concept answered some questions about how continents might move, but others remained. It was well known that convection works in liquids, but it had not been demonstrated in solids. Additionally, there was no certainty the process provided enough energy to move continents.

Violent processes underground were eventually identified as the cause of earthquakes.

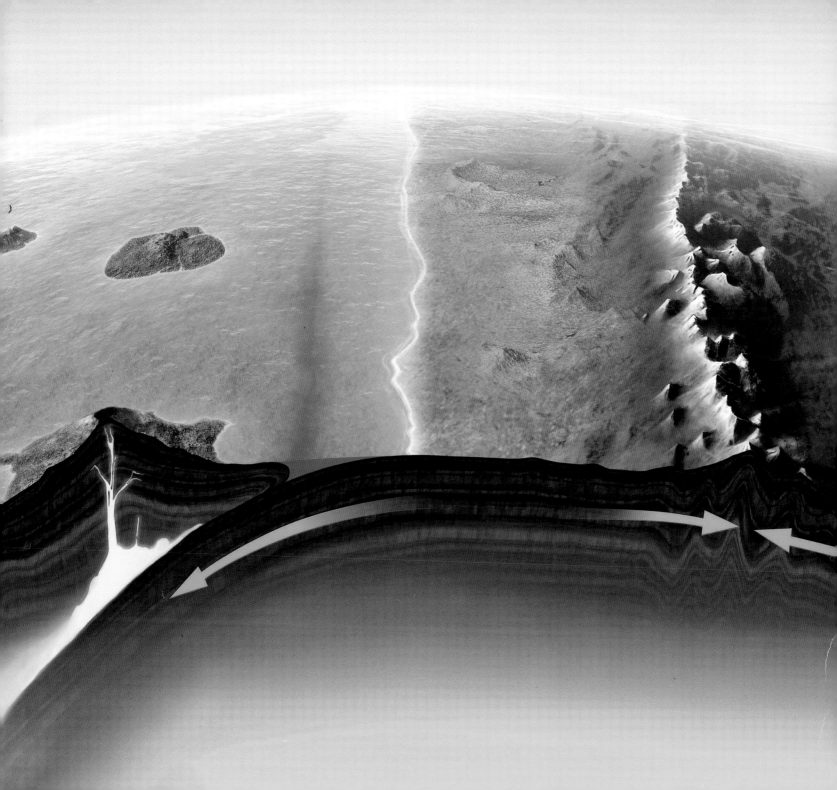

A RIFT IN ICELAND

Thingvellir was the site of Iceland's first parliament, the Althing, established in 930 CE. The valley where the parliament was located is also a part of the Mid-Atlantic Ridge. In this area, the North American Plate is pulling away from the Eurasian Plate, leaving a deep fissure visible above ground. The entire country of Iceland is being split by this fissure. The land has fallen approximately 130 feet (40 m), and the rift has spread approximately 230 feet (70 m).[2] Two earthquakes occurred in Iceland in 2000. In 2010, the Eyjafjallajökull volcano erupted and disrupted air travel due to the ash in the air. Ongoing volcanic activity with magma close to the surface provides Iceland with geothermal power.

New Technology Reveals Surprises

After World War II, technological advances developed during the war were put to work in seismology and geology. Magnetic sensors and depth-sounding devices, which use sound waves and their travel times to map the distance to the bottom of the ocean, were used to explore the ocean floor.

Scientists had assumed the ocean floors would be fairly smooth and the composition of the crust would be similar to that found on land. To their great surprise, scientists found the oceans contain huge mountains and deep trenches. The mountain ranges are thousands of feet high in some cases. Strung together, the ranges are nearly 37,000 miles (60,000 km) long and encircle Earth.[1] The mountains are known as the mid-ocean ridges. The ocean's deep trenches reach thousands of feet below the surface.

The scientists also thought Earth's crust under the oceans would be very thick as a result of sediment buildup.

But it was actually thin compared with what is seen above the seas. It is only a few miles thick, though it is much denser than the dry land.

These discoveries perplexed geologists, but more puzzling information was coming. Another technological tool, the magnetometer, was used by geologists after 1945. These devices measure the strength and direction of magnetic fields. Towing magnetometers over the ocean floor, geologists found an array of magnetic stripes. The seafloor is rich in basalt rock, which is formed by volcanoes. Basalt has a high concentration of iron. As the rock cooled after its formation, the iron compounds were magnetized and lined up with the magnetic field of Earth.

Scientists know the magnetic field of Earth has flipped numerous times in history. Iron-containing rocks on continents showed the reversal of Earth's magnetic field, so it appeared the rock of the ocean floor was also showing sections of rock indicating the opposite magnetic fields. Two British geologists, Frederick Vine and Drummond Matthews, proposed the magnetic properties of the basalt could be used to determine the direction of the magnetic field when the rock was formed. But why would the rock show so many stripes of rocks formed under a different magnetic field?

New Theory

The new discoveries forced geologists to come up with a theory that fit the information. The conclusion was that the seafloor is spreading apart. The stripes of magnetism showed the process taking place as new rock was formed. The rocks along the mid-ocean ridges were shown to be younger than the rock farther away. It seemed that new rock was being made and forced upward into the seafloor, but if the seafloor was expanding, it seemed as though the world would need to be getting larger as more rock was pushed up from the mantle. It should be expanding like a balloon that is being inflated.

Princeton University geologist Harry H. Hess proposed new crust was being formed at the mid-ocean ridges and then pushed away as more formed. The crust was eventually pulled down into the oceanic trenches where it was consumed in a recycling process. His theory explained why the ocean floor had a thinner crust than the dry land. Scientists had assumed the ocean floor would be heavily covered with sediment, which would compress into a thicker crust. However, if as Hess proposed, the floor was constantly being pushed up at the mid-ocean ridges by magma, stretched out across the floor, and finally consumed at the trenches, it did not have enough time to collect a heavy sediment load. Also, the presence of the magnetic stripes supported Hess's theory. The magnetic stripes occurred as each section was pushed out at the ridges, forming rock, and then was pushed across the floor by the next section being formed.

When Earth's polarity was oriented in a certain way, the rock had been magnetized in that direction. When the polarity reversed, the magnetization happened in a reversed direction. Moving outward from the ridge, the stripes

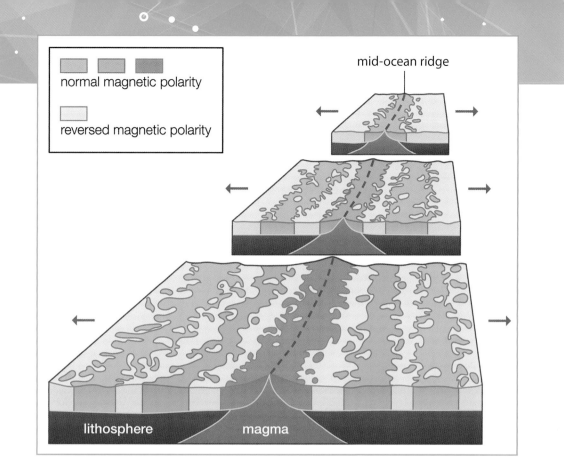

normal magnetic polarity

reversed magnetic polarity

mid-ocean ridge

lithosphere   magma

The magnetic properties of the seafloor provided crucial evidence supporting the theory that the seafloor spreads apart.

alternated between normal magnetic polarity and reversed magnetic polarity. This showed the seafloor was spreading over time. The new seafloor becomes part of the lithosphere, which includes the crust and the uppermost layer of the mantle.

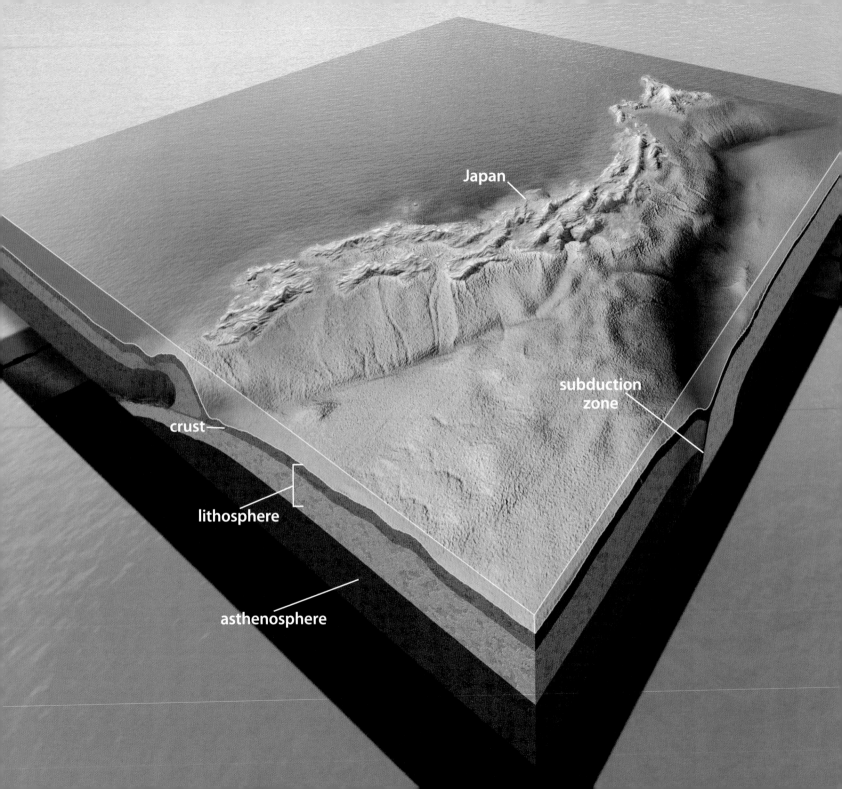

As more research was conducted, pieces of the puzzle began to take shape in a new theory similar to Wegener's continental drift. The new theory is called plate tectonics. It states the continents and the ocean floor are supported on the mantle of Earth in sections called plates. The plates cover Earth and collide with each other at plate boundaries. The most active areas for earthquakes and volcanoes are along these boundaries.

The strongest earthquakes happen where two plates meet in a subduction zone. In these spots, one plate sinks under the other. The plates get stuck against each other, and stress builds up. When the plates finally move past each other, the process releases enormous amounts of energy, creating powerful earthquakes.

Earthquakes Support Theory

As seismologists looked for support for the plate tectonic theory through the 1960s, two events enhanced their understanding of earthquakes. On May 22, 1960, the largest earthquake ever measured struck off the coast of Chile. The 9.5 magnitude quake killed more than 2,000 people, partly because of a tsunami that hit Chile and other areas, including Hawaii, Japan, and the West Coast of the United States. The rupture zone was estimated to be 620 miles (1,000 km) long.[3] The rip occurred where the oceanic Nazca Plate is being subducted under the continental South American Plate.

Zones where plates meet, including those near Japan, have frequent earthquakes and volcanoes.

The Tectonic Plates

This map of Earth shows major tectonic plate boundaries. During the last half of the 1900s, the sizes and shapes of the major plates were mapped. Once seismologists accepted the plate tectonics theory, they could predict where earthquakes were most likely to occur.

There are approximately 12 major tectonic plates making up Earth's crust, each up to 60 miles (100 km) thick. The plates float atop the melted rock making up the top layer of the mantle. They move slowly, at approximately 2 to 4 inches (5–10 cm) per year. This means there is little movement in the course of a human lifetime. But over millions or billions of years of such movement, the shape and arrangement of the continents have changed dramatically.

The descriptions of elastic waves and faults, the invention of the seismograph, the development of ways to measure earthquakes, and Wegener's continental drift theory all contributed to the modern understanding of plate tectonics. Each piece was a step to a more complete understanding of how Earth works.

This knowledge, combined with what was known of fault locations, led to more stringent building codes in earthquake-prone areas. That advance has saved lives and prevented property damage.

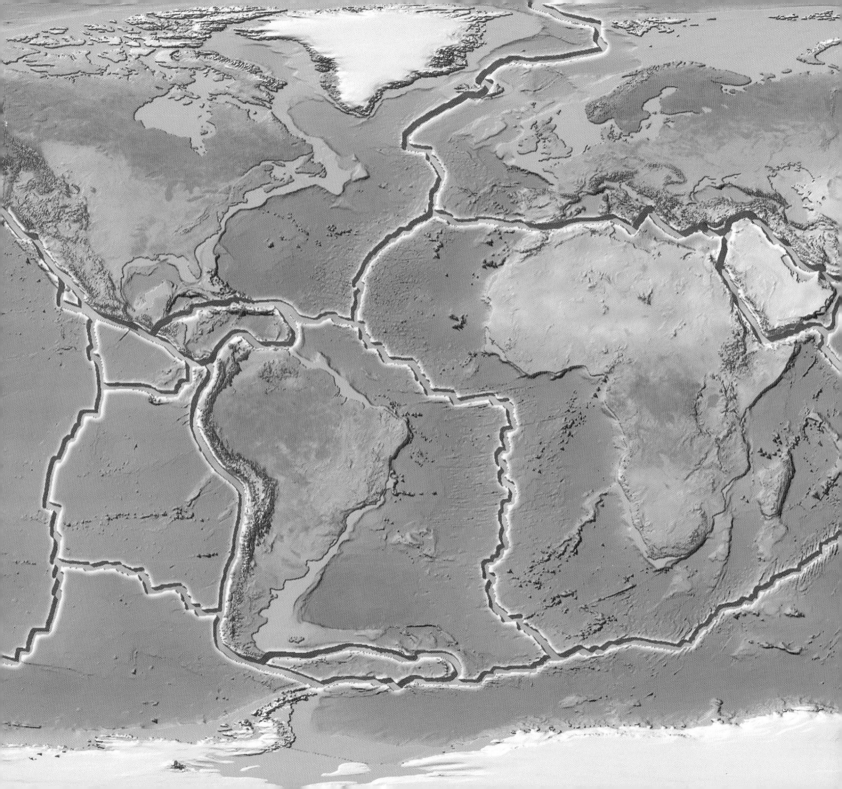

INTRAPLATE EARTHQUAKES

Earthquakes occur not only at plate boundaries but also in the middle of plates. For example, the most deadly earthquake ever hit in the middle of China in 1556. Approximately 800,000 people died when the quake struck.[8] Earthquakes that happen in the midwestern United States are not along a plate boundary. Seismologists believe these quakes occur at strain points inside plates.

On Friday, March 27, 1964, an earthquake struck Prince William Sound, Alaska. What was called the "Good Friday Earthquake" was measured at 9.2 magnitude. This made it the second most powerful earthquake known. The shaking lasted approximately 4.5 minutes.[4]

Altogether 129 people died, and the city of Anchorage suffered heavy property damage.[5] Schools, businesses, and a new six-story apartment building were completely destroyed. The quake also caused a tsunami that destroyed the town of Valdez and heavily damaged other cities. The Alaska quake even caused the Space Needle in Seattle, Washington, more than 1,200 miles (1,900 km) away, to sway.[6] Water swirled around in lakes and rivers as far away as Texas and Louisiana.

The earthquake was caused by subduction of the Pacific Plate under the North American Plate. Large sections of land moved vertically. Approximately 48,000 square miles (120,000 sq km) of seafloor and land dropped by several feet, and 60,000 square feet (5,600 sq m) rose.[7]

Earth's plates can also pull apart, creating a rift, such as the East African Rift Zone. The Red Sea formed by the separation of the African Plate and the Arabian Plate. Saudi Arabia has already ripped away from the African Plate. As the joint expands, the Red Sea may turn into the world's newest ocean. Volcanic activity can also increase along the rift as the pulling thins the crust. Seismologists and geologists now accept the theory of plate tectonics. Their focus has turned to predicting or preventing earthquakes.

RING OF FIRE

The Pacific Ocean is rimmed with the edges of plates. Many earthquakes and volcanoes occur in these areas. The region is known as the Ring of Fire. Mount Saint Helens, located in Washington State, is an active volcano. It last erupted in 1980. The volcano, along with frequent earthquakes, is sitting on the subduction zone where the North American Plate meets a small plate known as the Juan de Fuca. Other active volcanoes around the Ring of Fire include Mount Fuji in Japan, Mount Ruapehu in New Zealand, and Krakatoa, an island in Indonesia. Krakatoa suffered an eruption that completely destroyed the island in 1883. A new island is being formed there from volcanic activity.

Chapter Nine

Other Consequences
OF EARTHQUAKES

$$\frac{a+b}{a} = \frac{a}{b} = 1{,}618$$

Earthquakes do more than shake the ground and split it open. Throughout history, they have frequently been accompanied by other disasters, including tsunamis and landslides. The word *tsunami*, "harbor wave," comes from the Japanese language. Living on an island in an earthquake-prone area, the Japanese have been familiar with earthquakes and tsunamis since ancient times.

What Is a Tsunami?

Tsunamis strike after an earthquake occurs under the ocean. When the seafloor is thrust upwards by an earthquake, the water above that section is also propelled up, forming waves. The waves spread out in all directions and can travel up to 600 to 800 miles per hour (1,000 to 1,300 kmh)—as fast as an airplane.[1]

The raging waters of tsunamis can quickly multiply the damage caused by earthquakes.

As the waves cross the ocean, they appear small and people on ships hardly feel them. But as they approach land and the water becomes shallower, the waves grow in height and hit the shore with a great deal of energy. The water can rush far inland in a short time. After a tsunami ravaged Chile in 1960, ships were found nearly two miles (3 km) from the coast, carried by the onrushing water.[2]

Tsunamis cause even more damage when they surge back out to sea. The debris the water has scoured off of the land is carried along and can damage structures as it flows back into the ocean.

Sumatran Earthquake

On December 26, 2004, an earthquake ripped open a fault north of Sumatra, Indonesia. The seismic waves were incredibly complex because of the continuing release of energy as the fault tore open, almost like unzipping a zipper. Pulling a zipper apart requires energy that is first exerted at the top and continues downward. If a zipper is pulled open, the first teeth have already experienced the tear before the last teeth. The same thing can happen in earthquakes as they rip open along a long fault. Energy is released at the first point of the fault that ruptures, and it continues to be released as the rupture lengthens. The shock waves from the first energy release travel for several minutes before the energy of the end of the rupture is released, sending out more shock waves. The energy waves overlap and interfere with each other.

The earthquake came from the Indian Plate sliding under the Burma Plate. The fault was ripped open for nearly 600 miles (1,000 km), and the quake moved trillions of tons of rock under the ocean, causing an enormous tsunami.[4]

The beaches of Sumatra and the city of Banda Aceh were close to the epicenter of the earthquake, and a large tsunami surged ashore within 10 to 15 minutes. The tsunami swept people, buildings, cars, and trees out to sea.

Because of the Christmas holiday, many travelers were enjoying the beaches of Thailand, Sri Lanka, and India. They had no idea an earthquake off the coast of Sumatra would put them in danger. Some had felt the tremors, but they did not realize they would be affected.

PACIFIC TSUNAMI MUSEUM

The people of Hilo, Hawaii, are very familiar with tsunamis. On April 1, 1946, a tsunami generated by an earthquake near the Aleutian Islands of Alaska struck Hilo. There was no warning of the oncoming tsunami because a Coast Guard station in the Aleutians was destroyed before it could send the news. The Hilo waterfront was destroyed.

On May 23, 1960, 15 hours after a gigantic quake off the coast of Chile, a tsunami slammed ashore at Hilo Bay on the Big Island. Most of downtown Hilo was devastated, and 61 people lost their lives. Eight separate waves crashed ashore.[5] The Pacific Tsunami Museum in Hilo commemorates these events and other local tsunamis.

In a little over an hour, the coasts of Sri Lanka and Thailand were inundated by the tsunami. The area hit in Thailand was a tourist resort area. Thousands of people were pulled out to sea along with debris.

The tsunami continued to strike seashores around the Indian Ocean. In some places, the waves reached 50 feet (15 m) high before they crashed ashore. The waves hit a total of 11 countries. They traveled as far as 3,000 miles (5,000 km), causing damage on the shores of Africa.[6]

Approximately three hours after the earthquake, an aftershock measuring 7.1 occurred. In the next few days, more aftershocks greater than 6.0 happened.[7] The 2004 Sumatran earthquake was the third-largest earthquake in magnitude since 1900, and its tsunami killed more people than any tsunami in recorded history. It left approximately 286,000 people dead and another 1.7 million homeless.[8]

Japan Disaster

At 2:46 p.m. on Friday, March 11, 2011, an earthquake struck off the coast of northeastearn Japan. It was caused by a rupture between the Pacific and North American Plates at the Japan Trench subduction zone. The Pacific Plate is thrusting under the North American at a rate of 3.5 inches (8.9 cm) per year, moving at twice the rate of the plates sliding past each other in the San Andreas Fault.[9]

The December 2004 tsunami in Indonesia scoured huge sections of the coastal region.

The rip in the subduction zone was huge, at 180 miles (290 km) long and 50 miles (80 km) across. The depth of the hypocenter was approximately 15 miles (24 km) below the seafloor. People felt the severe shaking for three to five minutes, and the tremors were felt hundreds of miles away.[10] Some damage resulted from the shaking, but the worst was yet to come.

In eight minutes, a tsunami hit Sendai, a city of 1 million people.[11] Boats were shoved ashore, and the wave swamped the city and the airport. After the tsunami pulled back, boats and airplanes were mixed among the debris. Hundreds of people were dead and missing, including many who had been on trains that were swept away.

Kamaishi, a fishing port, is situated in a long, narrow valley leading down to the shore. Because of the danger of a tsunami funneling water up the valley, the town built a breakwater for protection. The project had taken 30 years and was barely finished when the 2011 tsunami hit.

The earthquake did little damage in Kamaishi, but tsunami sirens began wailing as soon as the shaking stopped. Many felt the breakwater would protect them, so they stayed where they were. When the tsunami arrived, its waves quickly overtopped the breakwater and swirled into the town, scouring away buildings, trees, and people. The breakwater was not high enough, but it did help somewhat. It slowed the

The Fukushima Daiichi nuclear power plant, inundated by the tsunami, released dangerous radiation into the environment.

tsunami rush, giving people time to escape. It also lessened the force of the water. Still, more than 1,000 people died, and the harbor area was demolished.[12]

The most serious tsunami effects were felt at the Fukushima Daiichi nuclear power plant. The power plant shut down automatically with the shaking of the earthquake, and the tsunami reached the plant 45 minutes later. A defensive breakwater had been built around the four nuclear reactor buildings, but it was much too short to defend against the large waves. The tsunami engulfed the breakwater and swirled into the plant. It flooded the emergency backup diesel generators that provided power for the cooling system for the reactors.

The plant's primary power source had been cut off by the earthquake, and now the tsunami had taken out the emergency power. Without power, the cooling systems for the nuclear reactors were dead, and the reactors began heating up. Engineers and plant personnel worked frantically to restore cooling systems, but three of the four reactors eventually exploded, releasing radioactivity into the atmosphere. The government declared a 12-mile (20 km) radius around the plant unsafe. Approximately 200,000 people had to evacuate and abandon their homes, not knowing if they would ever be able to return.[13]

TSUNAMI WARNINGS

Two centers run by the National Oceanic and Atmospheric Administration produce tsunami warnings after an earthquake happens under the sea. One, located in Hawaii, is called the Pacific Tsunami Warning Center and covers the Pacific Ocean. Another center provides warning for the eastern United States, Puerto Rico, Canada, and the Virgin Islands.

The centers receive notice from seismic networks that an undersea earthquake has occurred. Then they gather information from buoys around the world attached to the seafloor. These buoys contain sensors that measure the wave movement. Once a tsunami wave is suspected, warnings are issued for the areas that might be impacted. The warnings have saved countless lives.

By 2014, tsunami debris and makeshift memorials still littered the region around the power plant.

Like the fires that often start after earthquakes, tsunamis can cause hundreds of deaths and millions of dollars in damages. They bring an additional dimension of destruction to already-devastating earthquakes.

Chapter Ten

An Evolving
SCIENCE

$$\frac{a+b}{a} = \frac{a}{b} = 1,618$$

Through seismic studies, scientists have learned a wealth of information about the structure of Earth. Sometimes they traveled to quarries or mines when explosive blasts were scheduled to study the effects of the blasts and waves. But waiting for an earthquake or for quarry blasting took too long. A way to provoke seismic waves was needed, along with sensitive and portable seismographs. As early as 1913, scientists conducting experiments in Germany and the United States had theorized that seismic waves might be used to map underground geology. However, when World War I (1914–1918) began, much of this research was suspended.

Finding Oil and Gas

In 1916, John Karcher finished a degree in physics at the University of Oklahoma and headed for the University of Pennsylvania for graduate work. But once the United

Today's scientists use principles of seismology to build and analyze three-dimensional models of Earth's underground structure.

FRACKING AND EARTHQUAKES

In April 2014, the USGS released the news that Oklahoma had 109 quakes with magnitude 3.0 or greater in 2014.[1] This matched the total number of earthquakes of this power in Oklahoma in all of 2013. Scientists speculate the cause is the injection of water into wells for breaking rock layers to release oil and gas, as well as the subsequent disposal of the drilling fluid. This process is known as hydraulic fracturing or fracking.

Fracking is highly controversial. One side says fracking endangers the environment, even causing earthquakes. The other notes the earthquakes are mild and the United States needs the oil and gas that are produced. This debate will likely go on for years to come.

States entered the war in 1917, he started working for the US Bureau of Standards, learning to detect seismic waves to locate the enemy artillery that produced them. William Haseman, his professor at the University of Oklahoma, also joined the Bureau of Standards and worked with Karcher. Haseman realized this method could also be used to study the underground geologic structure of Earth. As seismic waves traveled through the ground, they were bent or reflected back according to the differing types of rock. Measuring the waves could give an indirect view of the rock structures below the ground. Once the war was over, Haseman and Karcher set up a company to use this technique to locate oil reserves. Equipment is placed down deep holes and sound waves are produced, causing seismic waves. The waves are detected and recorded. They develop into a pattern showing the underground rock layers and possible open areas that might contain oil, much like an X ray shows the inside structure of a body.

Similar methods are still used to locate oil and gas sources. A seismologist uses equipment to send seismic waves deep into the earth and seismographs to detect the waves' movement and convert it into electric signals. These signals can be interpreted to show if oil or gas reservoirs are present.

Detecting Nuclear Tests

After World War II, the United States and the Soviet Union began large-scale testing of nuclear weapons. Many of these tests took place underground, and seismographs around the world could detect them. The United States set up the Worldwide Standard Seismograph Network (WWSSN) to monitor nuclear testing by the Soviet Union. The WWSSN could detect where nuclear weapons had been tested and how big they were.

Seismographs can also detect other incidents that cause seismic waves. On August 12, 2000, the Russian submarine *Kursk* sank in the Barents Sea. Everyone on board died. At first, Russian officials did not want to reveal what caused the disaster. But seismographs in Norway had captured the sound of explosions. Underwater explosions show a different signature on seismographs than earthquakes. The truth came out that an explosion happened in one of the submarine's torpedo tubes, leading to a larger explosion that caused the sub to sink.

Can Earthquakes Be Predicted?

For years, scientists have sought to predict when big, damaging earthquakes are about to happen. Foreshocks can bring predictions of a large earthquake to follow,

Following the 2010 earthquake in Haiti, the USGS sent equipment and scientists to the area to help monitor future seismic activity.

but this only happens about half of the time. Other foreshocks are followed by nothing. Scientists cannot tell whether small quakes are foreshocks or simply small earthquakes. Seismologists have looked for other indicators for coming earthquakes, but the seemingly random timing of the events makes good forecasts impossible with current scientific knowledge.

The Earthquake Hazards Program was set up under the USGS to reduce earthquake dangers in the United States. While some of its money goes to prediction efforts, a large amount is directed to mitigating earthquake risks. One project is the Advanced National Seismic System, a program to install new earthquake monitoring equipment.

Reducing Risk

Since prediction has been an extremely difficult goal, seismologists, architects, and engineers have devoted their efforts to reducing the risk from devastating quakes. People in these fields often note that earthquakes do not kill people—buildings do. Other than from tsunamis, the majority of deaths from earthquakes come from collapsing buildings or falling materials.

Architects and engineers use techniques to reinforce buildings so they have a good chance of not collapsing in an earthquake. One method useful to reinforce buildings is attaching diagonal braces to the support girders. The braces provide strength in every direction, so even if an earthquake twists the girders or takes out a few of the reinforcement braces, the others can still support the building's weight.

Buildings are more likely to collapse if the first floor is not as strong and solid as the other floors. For example, apartment buildings often have parking garages on the first floor. Those floors must be carefully designed to provide the same strength as the sections above. If not, even the stronger areas will collapse when the columns in the parking garage give way.

Other structures must also be designed to be earthquake resistant. No structure is completely earthquake proof, but buildings, highway overpasses, and roads and bridges can be built in ways to mitigate damage. Engineers and architects build models of structures and test them on devices called shake tables to see if designs will hold up in an earthquake. They can then change designs if needed.

The field of seismology has taken dramatic steps forward in the past century. The diligent work of scientists has made it possible to study relatively rare events that often last no longer than a few minutes. Once the science behind earthquakes was established, researchers were able to use this knowledge to piece together the inner workings of Earth's structure. Wegener's theory of plate tectonics laid the groundwork for the modern understanding of our planet. The next great advance may be the prediction of earthquakes. Tomorrow's seismologists may unlock the secrets that make such predictions possible.

Architects and engineers can make existing buildings safer in a process known as seismic retrofitting.

Timeline

300s BCE Aristotle proposes early theories of how earthquakes work.

132 CE Zhang Heng invents the first seismograph.

1666 Robert Boyle and John Wallis investigate an earthquake in England.

1755 After a large earthquake and tsunami devastate Lisbon, Portugal, John Michell begins developing his elastic wave theory.

1855 A large earthquake in New Zealand provides evidence for the existence of faults that move during earthquakes.

$$\frac{b}{a} = \frac{a}{b} = 1,618$$

1856 Luigi Palmieri builds a seismograph that records the timing of earthquakes.

1857 Robert Mallet investigates an earthquake in Naples, Italy, and begins his experiments with elastic waves produced by underground explosions.

1885 Rayleigh waves are identified.

1906 The San Francisco, California, earthquake and fire kill thousands.

1912 Love waves are described; Alfred Wegener proposes his continental drift theory.

1935 Charles Richter and Beno Gutenberg develop the Richter scale.

1960 The most powerful earthquake ever known hits Chile.

1964 A huge earthquake strikes Prince William Sound, Alaska.

1960s–1970s Seismologists and geologists accept the plate tectonics theory.

1970s Hiroo Kanamori establishes the moment magnitude scale.

2004 A destructive earthquake occurs off the coast of Sumatra, and the tsunami it generates devastates shores around the Indian Ocean.

2010 On January 12, an earthquake strikes Port au Prince, Haiti; an earthquake shakes the coast of Chile on February 27.

2011 A powerful earthquake ruptures a fault off the coast of northeastern Japan. The following tsunami damages towns and a nuclear power plant.

Essential Facts

Seismographs

Seismographs show not only the magnitude and direction of earthquakes, but also the time they occurred and how long they lasted. This provides more data for seismologists to study when figuring out why earthquakes occur.

Magnitude Scales

Several scientists have developed scales to measure earthquake magnitude, making it easier to estimate earthquake damage and compare earthquakes with each other. The two that are best known are the Richter scale and the moment magnitude scale.

IMPACT ON SCIENCE

Seismology began thousands of years ago, but its findings have become accurate only in the last few centuries. Ancient thinkers tried to explain the shaking of the ground in ways that made sense to them, but their answers were often rooted in prescientific notions of the way the universe works. After the Scientific Revolution, scientists began collecting more hard data about quakes, taking detailed measurements and noticing the emergence of patterns in earthquake locations. The movement of seismic waves proved to be a useful tool in determining the composition of Earth's layers. In the 1900s, the development of plate tectonics answered questions about earthquakes that had been around for thousands of years.

KEY EARTHQUAKES

Several earthquakes throughout history have provided motivation for scientists and other thinkers to learn more about how these events happen. An earthquake that struck Pompeii, in ancient Rome, led ancient thinkers to ponder what could cause such events. The Lisbon earthquake of 1755 incited modern scientific interest in how earthquakes happen. Earthquakes in New Zealand in 1855 and San Francisco in 1906 led to a greater understanding of the connection between faults and earthquakes.

QUOTE

"Let us ask ourselves, therefore, what it is that stirs the earth to its foundation, what moves a mass of such weight, what it is that is stronger than the earth, and that in its violence can shake such a load."

—*Seneca*

$$\frac{a+b}{a} = \frac{a}{b} = 1{,}618$$

Glossary

aftershock

A less powerful earthquake following the main shock of an earthquake.

cardinal directions

North, east, south, and west.

continental drift theory

The idea proposed by Alfred Wegener that all the continents started as one mass and then moved apart.

elastic rebound

The theory that rocks behave in an elastic manner when stressed by a force.

elastic wave

A wave that moves through rock after receiving a stress, such as an earthquake.

epicenter

The point on Earth's surface directly above the hypocenter of an earthquake.

fault

A fracture in the ground with sides that can move in different directions.

foreshock

A less powerful earthquake that precedes the main shock of an earthquake.

hypocenter

The point where a fault begins to rupture; it is also called the focus.

intermediate directions

Northwest, northeast, southwest, and southeast.

liquefaction

The fluidlike behavior of water-saturated soil responding to the shaking of an earthquake.

mid-ocean ridge

A mountain range on the ocean floor formed by volcanic activity at a plate boundary.

oceanic trench

A depression in the seafloor where plates meet and one is forced under the other.

plate tectonics

The theory that continents and the ocean floor move on large sections or plates.

polarity

The orientation of a magnetic field.

primordial

Existing since the beginning of time.

rift

A split in the rocks of Earth's crust where the plates are pulling apart.

seismograph

A machine that measures the magnitude of an earthquake or other seismic event and also marks the time of the occurrence.

seismology

The study of earthquakes and other seismic phenomena.

subduction zone

An area where one plate is forced under another, leading to severe strain.

tsunami

A sea wave caused by displacement of water by an earthquake under the ocean.

Additional Resources

Selected Bibliography

Bolt, Bruce. *Earthquakes and Geological Discovery.* New York: Scientific American, 1993. Print

Brumbaugh, David S. *Earthquakes: Science and Society.* Upper Saddle River, NJ: Prentice Hall, 1999. Print.

Musson, Roger. *The Million Death Quake: The Science of Predicting Earth's Deadliest Natural Disaster.* New York: Palgrave, 2012. Print.

Further Readings

Kusky, Timothy M. *Earthquakes: Plate Tectonics and Earthquake Hazards.* New York: Facts on File, 2008. Print.

Simon, Seymour. *Earthquakes.* New York: Harper, 2012. Print.

Websites

To learn more about History of Science, visit **booklinks.abdopublishing.com**. These links are routinely monitored and updated to provide the most current information available.

For More Information

Pacific Tsunami Museum
130 Kamehameha Avenue
Hilo, Hawaii 96720
808-935-0926

http://earthquake.usgs.gov
The USGS website lists most recent earthquakes, data about past earthquakes, and daily earthquake facts. It also sponsors the Did You Feel It program to collect information from the public about local earthquakes. The site has a wealth of educational resources about earthquakes.

USGS National Center
USGS Headquarters
12201 Sunrise Valley Drive
Reston, Virginia 20192

http://www.tsunami.org/visitor.html
The museum provides programs about tsunamis, especially those that have struck in Hawaii. A self-guided tour provides stories and quotes from survivors of the April 1, 1946 tsunami. Educational programs and other events are listed.

Source Notes

Chapter 1. A Tale of Two Quakes

1. "Haiti Earthquake Facts and Figures." *Disasters Emergency Committee*. Disasters Emergency Committee, n.d. Web. 15 Sept. 2014.

2. "Earthquake Science: The Haitian Quake Explained." *Live Science*. Fox News, 13 Jan. 2010. Web. 15 Sept. 2014.

3. "Magnitude 7.0: Haiti Region Earthquake Summary." *Earthquake Hazards Program*. USGS, 7 May 2013. Web. 15 Sept. 2014.

4. Mary Harvey. "Earthquake in Haiti: An Eyewitness Account." *Junior Scholastic*. Junior Scholastic, 24 Jan. 2011. Web. 15 Sept. 2014.

5. Richard Pallardy. "Chile Earthquake of 2010." *Encyclopaedia Britannica*. Encyclopaedia Britannica, 19 Aug. 2014. Web. 15 Sept. 2014.

6. "Magnitude 8.8: Offshore Bio-Bio, Chile." *Earthquake Hazards Program*. USGS, 27 Feb. 2010. Web. 15 Sept. 2014.

7. Peter Granitz. "Four Years after Earthquake, Many in Haiti Remain Displaced." *NPR*. NPR, 12 Jan. 2014. Web. 15 Sept. 2014.

8. "Chile Earthquake: 'Nature Showed Us Her Fury.'" *BBC News*. BBC News, 28 Feb. 2010. Web. 14 Sept. 2014.

Chapter 2. Early Seismic Theories

1. Aristotle. "Meteorology." *MIT*. MIT, n.d. Web. 15 Sept. 2014.

2. Seneca. "Book VI: Which Treats of Earthquakes." *Seneca, Naturales Quaestiones*. Naturales Quaestiones, n.d. Web. 14 Sept. 2014.

3. Ibid.

4. Ibid.

5. "The Roman History of Ammianus Marcellinus." *Project Gutenberg*. Project Gutenberg, n.d. Web. 15 Sept. 2014.

6. Ibid.

7. Andrew Robinson. *Earthquake: Nature and Culture*. London, UK: Reaktion, 2012. Print. 62.

Chapter 3. Renaissance Science Tackles Earthquakes

1. "Lisbon, Portugal." *Earthquake Hazards Program*. USGS, 1 Nov. 2012. Web. 23 Sept. 2014.

2. Roger Musson. *The Million Death Quake*. New York: Palgrave, 2012. Print. 31–32.

3. "Rev. Charles Davy: The Earthquake at Lisbon, 1755." *Modern History Sourcebook*. Fordham University, 1998. Web. 15 Sept. 2014.

4. "Lisbon Earthquake of 1755." *Encyclopaedia Britannica*. Encyclopaedia Britannica, 2014. Web. 15 Sept. 2014.

5. Charles Lyell. *Principles of Geology*. New York: Appleton, 1853. Print. 559.

Chapter 4. Waves and Faults

1. Robert Mallet. *The First Principles of Observational Seismology*. London: Chapman and Hall, 1862. Print. 35.

2. Peter O. K. Krehl. *History of Shock Waves, Explosions, and Impact*. New York: Springer, 2009. Print. 321.

3. Roger Musson. *The Million Death Quake*. New York: Palgrave, 2012. Print. 41.

4. Ibid. 54–55.

Chapter 5. How Are Faults and Earthquakes Related?

1. David S. Brumbaugh. *Earthquakes: Science and Society*. Upper Saddle River, NJ: Prentice Hall, 2009. Print. 12.

2. Roger Musson. *The Million Death Quake*. New York: Palgrave. Print. 95.

3. "The San Francisco Earthquake, 1906." *Eyewitness to History*. Ibis Communications, n.d. Web. 22 Sept. 2014.

4. "Buildings Sank Like Quicksand: The Valencia Hotel." *The 1906 San Francisco Earthquake and Fire*. The Bancroft Library, 3 Jan. 2006. Web. 22 Sept. 2014.

5. "Room Three: A Firestorm from Hell." *The 1906 San Francisco Earthquake and Fire*. The Bancroft Library, 13 Apr. 2006. Web. 22 Sept. 2014.

6. "San Andreas Fault." *Encyclopaedia Britannica*. Encyclopaedia Britannica, 2014. Web. 22 Sept. 2014.

7. "Beno Gutenberg." *Encyclopedia.com*. Encyclopedia.com, 2008. Web. 22 Sept. 2014.

Source Notes Continued

Chapter 6. Magnitude and Intensity

1. "Earthquakes with 50,000 or More Deaths." *Earthquake Hazards Program*. USGS, 3 Dec. 2012. Web. 22 Sept. 2014.

Chapter 7. Continental Drift

1. Patrick Hughes. "Alfred Wegener." *Earth Observatory*. NASA, n.d. Web. 23 Sept. 2014.

2. Ibid.

3. Ibid.

Chapter 8. Plate Tectonics

1. "Mid-Ocean Ridges." *Woods Hole Oceanographic Institution*. Woods Hole Oceanographic Institution, n.d. Web. 23 Sept. 2014.

2. "Continental Drift." *Thingvellir National Park*. Thingvellir National Park, n.d. Web. 23 Sept. 2014.

3. "The Largest Earthquake in the World." *Earthquake Hazards Program*. USGS, 1 Nov. 2012. Web. 23 Sept. 2014.

4. "The 1964 Great Alaska Earthquake and Tsunamis— A Modern Perspective and Enduring Legacies." *Earthquake Science Center*. USGS, Mar. 2014. Web. 23 Sept. 2014.

5. "Largest Earthquake in Alaska." *Earthquake Hazards Program*. USGS, 18 Apr. 2014. Web. 23 Sept. 2014.

6. "The 1964 Great Alaska Earthquake and Tsunamis— A Modern Perspective and Enduring Legacies." *Earthquake Science Center*. USGS, Mar. 2014. Web. 23 Sept. 2014.

7. David S. Brumbaugh. *Earthquakes: Science and Society*. Upper Saddle River, NJ: Prentice Hall, 2009. Print. 158–159.

8. "Earthquakes with 50,000 or More Deaths." *Earthquake Hazards Program*. USGS, 3 Dec. 2012. Web. 22 Sept. 2014.

Chapter 9. Other Consequences of Earthquakes

1. David S. Brumbaugh. *Earthquakes: Science and Society*. Upper Saddle River, NJ: Prentice Hall, 2009. Print. 141.

2. Roger Musson. *The Million Death Quake*. New York: Palgrave, 2012. Print. 137.

3. Thucydides. "The History of the Peloponnesian War." Trans. Richard Crawley. *Project Gutenberg*. Project Gutenberg, 7 Feb. 2013. Web. 23 Sept. 2014.

4. "The Deadliest Tsunami in History?" *National Geographic News*. National Geographic, 7 Jan. 2005. Web. 23 Sept. 2014.

5. "The 1960 Tsunami, Hilo." *Hawaiian Volcano Observatory*. USGS, 26 Mar. 1998. Web. 23 Sept. 2014.

6. "The Deadliest Tsunami in History?" *National Geographic News*. National Geographic, 7 Jan. 2005. Web. 23 Sept. 2014.

7. "Magnitude 9.0 Sumatra-Andaman Islands Earthquake FAQ." *Earthquake Hazards Program*. USGS, 17 Mar. 2011. Web. 23 Sept. 2014.

8. Ibid.

9. Francie Diep. "Fast Facts about the Japan Earthquake and Tsunami." *Scientific American*. Scientific American, 14 Mar. 2011. Web. 23 Sept. 2014.

10. Jenny Marder. "Japan's Earthquake and Tsunami: How They Happened." *PBS NewsHour*. PBS, 11 Mar. 2011. Web. 23 Sept. 2014.

11. "Japan Earthquake: Tsunami Wave Sweeps Sendai Airport." *BBC News*. BBC, 11 Mar. 2011. Web. 23 Sept. 2014.

12. Roger Musson. *The Million Death Quake*. New York: Palgrave. Print. 137–139.

13. Pete Norman. "Japan: 200,000 Evacuated From Near Reactors." *Sky News*. Sky, 13 Mar. 2011. Web. 23 Sept. 2014.

Chapter 10. An Evolving Science

1. Jim Efstathiou Jr. "Oklahoma Swamped by Surge in Earthquakes Near Fracking." *Bloomberg News*. Bloomberg, 8 Apr. 2014. Web. 24 Sept. 2014.

Index

Advanced National Seismic System, 95
Alaska earthquake, 78
Ammianus Marcellinus, 21
Aristotle, 16, 18, 21, 29

body waves, 35–36
    P waves, 36, 44
    S waves, 36, 44
Boyle, Robert, 24, 26
building codes, 11, 54, 56, 76

Chile, 8, 10–11, 75, 82, 83
China, 21, 22, 60, 78
continental drift, 62, 65, 67, 75, 76

Davy, Charles, 28
de Rossi, Michele, 52

Earth's layers, 51, 76
    core, 46, 51
    crust, 40, 46, 51, 70–71, 72, 76, 79
    mantle, 51, 72, 76
Earthquake Hazards Program, 95
earthquakes
    aftershocks, 8, 10, 35, 85

epicenter, 10, 11, 35, 44, 54, 57, 83
foreshocks, 13, 46, 75, 93, 94
hypocenter, 40, 86
intensity, 52, 54, 57
magnitude, 43, 52, 54, 56, 57–58, 75, 85, 92
prediction, 13, 76, 79, 93–95, 96
ruptures, 39, 40, 75, 83, 85
elastic rebound, 51
elastic waves, 29–31, 32, 34, 35, 38, 43, 76

faults, 38–40, 43, 47, 49, 51, 58, 76, 82–83
Fernandez, Paulina, 11
fire, 19, 21, 27, 29, 31, 49, 60, 89
Flamsteed, John, 26
Forel, François-Alphonse, 52
four elements, 19
fracking, 92
Fukushima Daiichi nuclear power plant, 87–88

Galitzin, Boris, 42
Greece, 14, 16, 18, 82
Gutenberg, Beno, 51, 56, 57, 58

Haiti earthquake, 6, 8, 10–11, 60
Haseman, William, 92
Hess, Harry H., 72
Hilo, Hawaii, 83
Holmes, Arthur, 68

Iceland, 70
intraplate earthquakes, 78
ISC Bulletin, 49

Japan, 16, 42, 58, 60, 75, 79, 80, 85–88
Jean-François, Regine, 8

Kanamori, Hiroo, 58
Kant, Immanuel, 29
Karcher, John, 90, 92

landslides, 35, 80
Lawson, Andrew, 49
Lehmann, Inge, 46
Lick Astronomical Observatory, 46
liquefaction, 47
Lisbon earthquake, 27–29, 31
Love, A. E. H., 36, 38
Lyell, Sir Charles, 38–39

magnetism, 42, 71, 72–73
magnetometer, 71
Mallet, Robert, 32, 34–35, 39
Matthews, Drummond, 71
Mercalli, Giuseppe, 54
Michell, John, 29–31
Milne, John, 42, 44, 49
Missouri earthquakes, 35
myths, 16

Naples earthquake, 34, 35
National Earthquake Information
   Center, 49
National Oceanic and Atmospheric
   Administration, 88
nuclear testing, 93

ocean floor, 70–71, 72–73, 75, 79,
   80, 86

Pacific Tsunami Museum, 83
Palmieri, Luigi, 40
Pangaea, 64
plate tectonics, 68, 70–73, 75, 76,
   78–79, 96
Poseidon, 14

Rebeur-Paschwitz, Ernst von, 42
Reid, Harry Fielding, 49, 51
Richter, Charles, 56, 57–58
Richter scale, 58
Ring of Fire, 79
Rossi-Forel scale, 52
Royal Society, 26

San Andreas Fault, 47, 49, 51, 85
San Francisco earthquake, 46–47, 49
scientific instruments, 26, 36, 42, 54
Scientific Revolution, 22, 24
seismic waves, 35, 42, 46, 82, 90, 92
seismograph, 41–42, 43, 44, 52, 54, 56,
   57, 76, 90, 92–93
Seneca, 19–21
Shide Circulars, 42, 49
sound waves, 30–31, 32, 37, 38, 70, 92
Strabo, 18
Strutt, John William, 37
subduction zone, 75, 78, 79, 86
Sumatra earthquake, 60, 82–83, 85
surface waves, 35, 36–38
   Love waves, 36, 38
   Rayleigh waves, 37–38

tectonic plate boundaries, 75, 76, 78
Thales of Miletus, 16–17, 20
thermometer, 26
Thingvellir, 70
Thucydides, 82
tsunami warning, 88
tsunamis, 10, 11, 28–29, 60, 75, 78, 80,
   82, 83, 85, 86–89, 95

US Geological Survey, 49, 57, 92

Vine, Frederick, 71
volcanoes, 18, 19, 29, 31, 35, 51, 70, 71,
   75, 79

Wallis, John, 26
weather, 24, 26
Wegener, Alfred, 64, 65, 67, 75, 76, 96
World War I, 90
World War II, 67, 70, 93

Zhang Heng, 21, 22

About the Author

Roberta Baxter is the author of more than 25 books and numerous magazine articles for students ranging from kindergarteners to young adults. She specializes in writing about science and history, including biography and the history of science. Her background includes a degree in chemistry. She currently lives in Colorado.

$$\frac{a+b}{a} = \frac{a}{b} = 1.618$$